The Exorcist and the Possessed

First Published 1974

Printed in England by
Chapel River Press (IPC Printers), Andover
and published by
James Pike Ltd, St. Ives, Cornwall

50p

[illegible]

THE EXORCIST AND THE POSSESSED

by

CHRISTOPHER NEIL-SMITH

JAMES PIKE LTD

St. Ives, Cornwall

CONTENTS

INTRODUCTION

What is Exorcism! Is it fiction, fancy or fact?

To exorcise is to drive away, draw away or cleanse evil from people or places. Many people wrongly assume that it is purely a medieval ritual applied to haunted houses. Actually the exorcising of people is both ancient and modern; it was used in the ancient world and practised by Jesus himself. It has reappeared in the modern world with a startling new significance.

A recent novel THE EXORCIST is about an eleven year old girl 'possessed' by Satan. The author takes us through neurology and psychiatry but turns her over to exorcism. Is this fantastic? No. I have myself as a practising exorcist had a case of a girl of ten sent to me for exorcism because her own doctor considered she was 'possessed'. She too had been through psychiatry and neurology without effect.

I was asked to appear with the author, William Blatty, on Thames Television in Eamonn Andrews "Today" programme when THE EXORCIST was published in England. I was asked to explain what exorcism was and whether the novel reflected the facts. Whilst THE EXORCIST novel and recent film produced from it reveal the stark reality of possession in its horrific form, the novelistic embellishment surrounding them obscures rather than explores the actual evidence for possession.

Possession and exorcism were discussed in a "Man Alive" B.B.C. television programme in which both William Sargent, a psychiatrist, and I appeared. In his recent book entitled MIND POSSESSED, William Sargent gives a fascinating study of the phenomena of possession, but he fails to recognise that the exorcist actually expels external evil forces from a person and is not primarily concerned like the psychiatrist with projections of the mind or excitation of the emotions.

I have myself done 2,200 exorcisms since I first filmed an exorcism on television four years ago. Since that first film I have done thirty TV and Radio broadcasts for various parts of the world on exorcism—C.B.S. and A.B.C. (U.S.A.), C.B.C. (Canada), R.A.I. (Italy), Belgian Television, Swiss, West German and Africa Radio. Articles have appeared in the Press in U.S.A., Canada, Australia, South Africa and China as well as Holland, Belgium and Germany, showing a widespread interest in exorcism.

In this book I have endeavoured to explain by description rather than definition my own experience as an Exorcist in dealing with people from all over the world. In the first chapter I have described my own method of diagnosis—discernment through vibrations—and I have differentiated between evil as commonly conceived and what is actually perceived as evil. In the second chapter I have examined the different conditions caused by demonic attack in contrast to those which are psychological revealing the state of being possessed as an actual fact of experience. In the third chapter, I have described the powers of witchcraft and black magic as an objective force, showing the universal need for exorcism. In the last chapter, I have described the power of God to re-create new men and women for a new age.

Exorcism is not just fiction with novelistic embellishment—it is a fact of human experience—an answer to human need in the present age.

CHRISTOPHER NEIL-SMITH

Acknowledgements

I am most grateful to the Archbishop of Canterbury, Dr. Michael Ramsey, for his interest regarding this book and also to Bishop John Robinson for his advice on New Testament Greek words.

I am also grateful to Dr. R. D. Laing and Dr. Frank Lake for their observations on certain psychological conditions and also to the late Leonard Brice for his comments on legal matters. My thanks are also due to Leslie Giddens, Deaconess Halm and my son David for perusing the manuscripts, to James Pike for undertaking publication, to John Harper for inserting subtitles, to Alicia Dean who is seen being exorcised on the back cover and to June Geers and my wife, Dorothea for typing the manuscript.

CHRISTOPHER NEIL-SMITH

CHAPTER 1

WHY EVIL? VIBRATIONS

Not an idea—A force

What is evil? Is it all in the mind? Is it an idea or a force? This book is written with the intention of illustrating that evil is recognised for what it is by those who have experienced it in their daily lives. That is why I have used the phrase, 'evil forces', as well as 'evil spirits'. To decry evil is a failure to face facts.

Up till recently there has been a trend to treat the devil as a joke. John Robinson says "he has turned into a semi-comic figure".* It is therefore all the more surprising that a new and sinister form of violence under a man calling himself 'Satan', of the 'Satan's Slaves', should have come from the U.S.A.** In a TV discussion on Malcolm Muggeridge's "Question Why—Why Evil?", I pointed out that I could feel evil as an actual force in exorcisms and John Lennon took up my point by calling evil a 'form of energy'. It was very interesting that the 'pop' personality for thousands of young people should recognise evil in this way. His point is borne out by the fact that a teenager who had been mixed up in drugs and witchcraft told me after exorcism that it was as if a force of energy had left him, and he suddenly felt terribly tired. It seems to me that we should interpret evil as an actual force rather than an abstract idea if it is to have any sig-

* EXPLORATION INTO GOD, Robinson, pp. 41, 52, 53.
** MODERN WITCHCRAFT (see Chap. VII), Smyth.

nificance of meaning for the modern world. Young people, particularly nowadays, tend to become aware of evil through facing the stark reality of it in their own experience, rather than analysing it in abstraction.

Bad vibrations

Billy Graham says "Everywhere you go today, the young are complaining about bad vibrations. Bad vibrations have shaken our youth."* It was claimed that bad vibrations came from Manson during the 'Satan's Slaves' trials, and these could be felt by a number of people in the court room. Actually it is bad vibrations that an exorcist can perceive when he is interviewing a person for exorcism. Such a vibration has been described by a psychiatrist as a 'perception into the unconscious'. It is a modern way of diagnosing whether evil is affecting a person, and differentiating between what is diabolical and purely psychological. It is in line with the modern outlook in communication whereby Marshal McLuhan emphasises 'percept' rather than 'concept', directly perceiving a reality rather than conceptualising about it. The important point about 'vibrations' is that they can be perceived by a number of people simultaneously and therefore have an objective reality, and are not purely subjective to the consciousness of a particular individual. For instance, when members of the Press were interviewing me with an actor and actress concerning strange happenings in their house, the actress asked me whether I felt 'vibrations'. It was a fact that both she and I perceived bad vibrations emanating from the actor, and this later led to an exorcism because he admitted having outbreaks of violence during which he felt 'possessed'. It is a curious fact that some people who request to see me for exorcism reveal no vibrations, and after investigation I have found that they really need psychiatric treatment. Others are reluctant to acknowledge any suggestion of evil, and yet I have perceived bad vibrations

* THE JESUS GENERATION, Graham, p. 63.

through an interview, and it has subsequently led to the necessity for exorcism.

When I mentioned on the same programme that Black Magic was rampant in this country and quoted a case where a man seduced a girl and then attempted to strangle her, I was approached by five national newspapers in a couple of days. Dom Robert Petitpierre reckons that there are about four hundred Black Magic groups in this country and at least one in every university.* A psychiatrist recently said to me that there was a driving force—evil—which entered a person through seduction and destruction, which he recognised could not be treated by psychiatry and that is why certain psychiatrists are sending patients to priests.

In U.S.A., when United States Congress (in 1955) authorised a comprehensive study to 'analyse and evaluate the needs and resources of the mentally ill', it was revealed that the largest number of those actually seeking help (42%) turned to clergymen, whereas only 18% turned to psychiatrists.**

The Devil's back

John Robinson, when writing in the sixties, may well have been right when he claimed that the words "God, the Devil and the supernatural" had suffered a severe loss of reality. However, in the seventies the wind has changed, or the tide has turned, if you like,—and there has been a curious increase of interest in the supernatural. For instance, the very wide circulation of the recently published magazine "Man, Myth and Magic", described as an illustrated encyclopedia of the supernatural, is evidence of such an interest. Also, strange though it may seem, I have had quite a few invitations to speak on exorcism at both ancient and modern universities within the last few years, often to secular societies, and I have been surprised at the students' reactions and questions. I expected and prepared to meet arguments against

* "Growing Point," Times Interview, April 26th, 1972.
** Clinical Theology, Lake, p. 4.

exorcism on rational or scientific grounds. These arguments did not come because of the strange fascination there appears to be for this subject, which would have been considered medieval twenty or even ten years ago. Oddly enough, when I spoke to doctors and clergy, it was the doctors, like the secular students, who showed far more interest than the clergy and theological students. I was asked to do an exorcism on "24 Hours" television long before I appeared on a religious programme, and the "Sunday Times" interviewed me long before the "Church Times". I only point this out to illustrate the fact that the wider world realises the need to combat evil in whatever form, whilst the Church as a whole is far too reticent and reluctant to recognise its function to exorcise. For instance, a girl desired to be liberated from a witches' coven to which she had been attached for eight years. She approached five priests, three Roman Catholic and two Anglican, but admitted that none of them were willing or able to exorcise her. After I had exorcised her, she renounced her former practices and received the sacraments.

Recently, an American actor flew from New York to see me because of a witch-force he said had been put on him, and claimed that he found release and relief through exorcism. B.B.C. "Nationwide" filmed this exorcism and in the TV interview he mentioned that he had been to Roman Catholic priests in Italy and Spain, as well as psychiatrists in New York, but they could not help him.

How I found the gift of discernment

I have often been asked how I became interested in the subject of Exorcism. Originally, I had been practising the Healing Ministry through the Laying on of Hands, and I was approached by a man who asked for healing. This man subsequently turned out to be an unfrocked priest, who had been practising Black Magic and as I tried to heal him, I felt the impact of an evil force come upon me. It affected me in various ways, like lack of concentration and also lack of sleep, and I went in this condition to the late Rev. Gilbert Shaw, who, in fact, removed this oppressive force from me by exorcism. It was then, that I was in fact 'saved to serve' and he trained me subsequently to use exorcism for others. This was not a technical training in the sense of technology, but training in a spiritual way based on the ancient mystics particularly the writings of St. John of the Cross. I had to learn spiritual detachment. I had to be quite clear that if I was to be of any value as an exorcist, that my own sense of perception must be completely dulled, and what I discerned or diagnosed in people whom I interviewed was the evil force picked up from them and not my own imagination.

Vibrations

This method of discernment is through 'vibrations'. People often think that vibration is a matter of conjuring up imagination or feeling. Actually vibrations in this connection are very much along the lines that we would think of in terms of Physics. For instance, vibrations sometimes cause the hanging lights at the back of the church to rattle during an exorcism. An engineer pointed out to me that these vibrations could be due to a force of energy coming through the church from the person who has been exorcised. Also, on rare occasions, I have done exorcisms through the vibrations of the telephone. I have done exorcisms over the telephone to one man in New York, and to another in Hamburg and both claimed that they felt a vibration which gave them relief. The vibrations that I discern in an interview usually reach a climax when I take the person into church for exorcism, and then subside when the force is released. This vibration comes through the hands, and it does cause a certain vibration in the person and surrounding the person. This is not a psychic reaction, but the action of the Holy Spirit driving out the evil spirits; it is, as I understand, the gift of discerning of spirits, which I will refer to in more detail in a later chapter. A doctor told me that he can take 'sensitivity' tests like 'IQ' tests, and a person who has a high sensitivity, which he can measure, can perceive atmospheres of good and evil. The 'Hippies' talk of good and bad vibrations,—this is expressing a profound truth, and something which our modern age is coming to recognise through a deeper perception and a more sensitive awareness. When people sometimes say that they do not believe in ghosts or spirits, it could well be due to the fact that they have a low sensitivity, if they were tested, and what they cannot perceive they tend to decry.

Types of vibration

Now vibrations take various forms, and can be distinguished by certain types of sensation. For instance, a vibration which reveals an evil force is perceived by a 'sharp sting'*, whilst a vibration which reveals a good influence is perceived by a gentle tingling. In the same way, the Holy Spirit gives 'warmth', particularly through healing,—a real life giving spirit; whilst coldness is experienced in the presence of discarnate or departed spirits or ghosts. The vibration experienced in an exorcism is like the 'rushing mighty wind' experienced at Pentecost.

A well known New Theologian recently sent me a high powered scientist whom he considered a case of possession. Now this scientist, full of grave suspicions and mental reservations, accepted the need for exorcism because vibrations might reveal an 'objective force' which was causing violence. After the exorcism, this scientist reluctantly but firmly acknowledged that the evil force had dissolved. No doubt some people would still say that my mind was obsessed by this idea, and I would look for this in all sorts of people whether it existed or not, or even whether it was my imagination or not. Actually nothing could be further from the truth because I have perceived vibrations at times when I have been least expecting it and when my mind has been occupied with something quite different. For instance, I was looking round an old country house on holiday with a guide, when I suddenly felt a vibration and the guide subsequently mentioned that there

* "By the pricking of my thumbs, something wicked this way comes." Macbeth Act IV Sc. I.

had been a ghost where I had felt it. On another occasion, I was attending a conference on a totally different topic, and suddenly felt a vibration in the midst of a group of people. I immediately dismissed the idea, thinking to myself that I had imagined it, when a man approached me and asked me for exorcism as he had read about me in the Press. I only give these illustrations to show that such a vibration is a sign which reveals an objective force, and is no way dependent upon one's own thoughts or feelings. I know at least two other priests who also perceive such vibrations which help them to discern spirits for exorcism.

Like a water diviner

Once when I was asked to lay a ghost at a London flat, I went round the rooms first and told the occupants that I felt vibrations in five of the rooms, but not in the other three. They then told me that the ghost had been seen or felt in the five rooms I mentioned, but not in the other three. This was a clear indication that my vibrations related to the evidence from independent statements made by three other people who had seen or felt the ghost. I have been described as working like a water diviner:

> "*He uses his hands instead of a twig. If there is an evil force, he feels it in his hands as a tingle or sharp sting. After commanding the evil spirit to depart, he makes the sign of the Cross and lays his hands on the possessed person and as he does so he feels a very strong vibration which shakes the pair of them until the evil has gone. It appears that one is having a struggle with the person but it is not that at all. It is the evil force in the person having received the impact of the power of God through my hands," he explained.**

Exorcism on TV

Some people seemed to have grasped some strange ideas from my TV films of exorcism, one described it as violent, because they do not understand what is actually happening—it is the involun-

* Daily Mirror Magazine, January 31st, 1970, p. 21.

tary action of the hands moved by the Holy Spirit in order to remove the evil forces, and the exorcist is an instrument through whom the power comes. Others have described this as sensational, but I venture to suggest that if they had seen Jesus cast out the legion of demons into the herd of swine they would have considered that sensational or violent. A one time Chairman of B.B.C. "Critics" saw this TV programme and said he considered it a good documentary but it never struck him as at all sensational. A B.B.C. producer told me that a demonstration of this kind often had a far greater impact on the public than a discussion. It seems to me that the views of such experts only go to show that to call this kind of exorcism sensational or violent, is due to prejudice or ignorance rather than considered or informed opinion. An exorcism is, in a sense, rather like an operation and the exorcist like the surgeon has to be detached. It may seem strange to see an operation on television, because it is new to many people to see it at all, but it is all part of modern life which people have come to accept in a perfectly ordinary way. The Church like the medical profession should have nothing to hide in an age when openness is expected by the general public. It is the occult which has kept its secrets to itself, although even witches are now coming out into the open. The Church can often show its witness through exorcism on TV to people in their homes who would never enter a church in the ordinary way, and such evidence can be easily shown by the letters and telephone calls I have received through TV, Radio and Press from hundreds of people who have had no living connection with any Church from all over the country and from other parts of the world.

Good publicity

Archbishop William Temple used to say that the Press often reported what he said on economic and social issues, but left out what he said about spiritual matters. John Robinson recently stated that in contrast to Temple's day, the Press were now just as interested in fundamental issues as social or political issues.

John Robinson referred particularly to the interest given to his "Honest to God" and his reinterpretation of the Image of God. In some small way, there has also been a similar interest in evil spirits and the devil in the Press. For instance, when I appeared in a juvenile court trying to defend a boy who had set fire to a school on the grounds that he was possessed, I rather naturally thought that nothing would appear in the Press. On the contrary, I was approached by Radio, TV and Press within a matter of hours. Not only was the interest in this country, but through the United Press International there were comments in numerous papers throughout U.S.A. and Canada. I was asked to do a hot-line broadcast to Canada over the telephone for a programme in Toronto, a newstape for C.B.S. in New York, and interviewed by the "Sidney Morning Herald" from Australia.

New image for the devil

What surprised many people was the fact that in an age when the Church seemed to many rather a dead letter that the Press, TV and Radio should be so interested in a fundamental spiritual matter. Perhaps Harvey Cox, the American sociologist, was right when he spoke of the function of the Church as a cultural exorcist? The Daily Mirror recently asserted that according to a recent survey more than half of Britain believes in the devil.* However, it is not merely belief in the devil but a recognition of the stark reality of evil that is really important. It is here again that we have to see that percept is more relevant than concept. Through experience of evil within their midst, many people come to perceive the fact of evil without conceptualising about it. All sorts of people have requested exorcism for the evil they are encountering without necessarily accepting the idea of a personal devil. In the same way as it is necessary to reinterpret the image of God so it is also necessary to reinterpret the image of the devil, so that it is possible for people to accept evil as a fact in our lives

* Op. cit. Daily Mirror Magazine, January 31st, 1970, p. 21.

and an issue for our time. A professor pointed out to me that there were many people who showed a widespread concern about evil, but might never accept the idea of a personal devil. Far from attempting to deny the devil and the demons, I am attempting to reinterpret the image of the devil and reassert the principle of evil. In the same way as the new Confirmation (Series II) uses 'renounce evil' instead of 'renounce the devil', so it seems more natural to speak of evil forces rather than evil spirits. Evil has been described as a causal force and if we are to regard it in this sort of way then our whole mode of thinking about evil will have to be radically altered.

Evil is not—cricket

John Robinson calls himself a radical, and I believe it is necessary to take a radical view of evil to show its significance in the modern world. If one is to hold a radical view of evil, then it will be necessary to differentiate between expressions of evil and things which are evil in themselves. For instance, recently unemployment was described as an evil. As I see it, this seems to confuse the meaning of the word. Unemployment is purely a defect in the structure of society but not evil in itself, although evil intentions of employers or employees may cause unemployment. It is important that political, social and religious prejudices should not be allowed to obscure a fundamental issue. Why then should a rugby or cricket match between a South African team and an English (or Australian) team be considered evil? It may well be true that the principles of racial discrimination are inherently evil, but the Cricket Council had no intention of supporting this in inviting the South African team to England in 1970.

The Cricket Council later issued a special statement "Why the '70 Tour?" from which I quote:

> "*However much the Cricket Council may* deplore the policy of apartheid *in South Africa, its responsibility is to long term well-being of cricketers and cricket wherever it is played. It was*

therefore encouraging to learn that the South African Association had announced that they intend to select future touring teams on merit irrespective of class, creed and colour. It cannot be over-emphasised that the South African Cricket Association representatives have stressed again and again that they do not endorse any policy of apartheid in sport . . . *It is felt that encouragement not isolation is what is needed to ensure that further progress can be made.*"*

New Protestants

Unfortunately, as we now know, the South African tours to England and Australia have both been abandoned, largely due to protesters, whom we might call the 'New Protestants'. One of the leaders, David Sheppard, now Bishop of Woolwich, caused a special meeting of the M.C.C. to be called to discuss the matter, and later became Chairman of the Fair Cricket Campaign in an attempt to stop the tour because of its effect on community relations. Like the Protestants of old who objected by protesting loudly at services against ritual practices, the New Protestants have changed their venue to rugby football and cricket grounds. No doubt, like the Protestants of every age, they hold sincere convictions, but likewise they protest too much. Protestants have always been in danger of overstating the case, and the South African tour was no exception. The discrepancy in David Sheppard's argument about Jesus turning the money changers out of the temple in a demonstration is the fact that the money changers were themselves guilty of trading in the temple. The South African cricketers were *not* themselves applying apartheid. The Archbishop of York, after his visit to South Africa, put the matter in perspective when he said:

"*I think it is an awful pity when politics get into sport. The motives of the demonstrators may be praiseworthy but their methods are not. I personally believe it has all got out of hand.*"**

* "Why the '70 Tour?" A pamphlet sent to all members of M.C.C.
** A DAY IN THE LIFE OF GOD, De la Noy, p. 78.

In my letter to the Times* and at the M.C.C. A.G.M. I pointed out that I ministered to an African group drawn from various parts of Africa and residing in various parts of North London, and that many of them had misgivings about the demonstrations. One of them said to me, "You English do not understand us Africans. Your protests will not help us. It will only make our position in this country more difficult, and harden the government's attitude in South Africa." It was in May 1970 that I noticed in our group one African with his head bandaged. I discovered that he had been attacked by his landlord, and two others were thrown out of their lodging in the same week. Another African in the Group said to me, "We have no quarrel with the young sportsmen. They are being victimised because of their government." With the full backing of this African Group, I wrote to the Secretary of the M.C.C. suggesting that a few members of the South African team might like to visit this African Group in Hampstead when they came to Lords. Mr. S. C. Griffith thanked me for what he described as a "very Christian gesture" but it was impossible to pursue it because the South African team never came. Many people fail to recognise that the real evil is in racial strife, not sport, and they are sometimes blinded to the racialism in our midst by the protests they make or read in the newspapers. It is also sad that some of those who demonstrate actually cause evil—strife and violence in the name of the Prince of Peace.

Evil not institutional

> "*The deifying or rather idolising of the particular form that these institutions took in some particular age—is a dangerous and demonic perversion.*"**

If these words were applied to the institution of the Orange Order in Northern Ireland, and the perpetuation of this Order by

* May 4th, 1970.
** Growing into Union, Buchanan, Mascall, Packer, Willesden, p. 97.

annual parades commemorating the Battle of the Boyne, 1690, then they would express a profound and penetrating insight into the present situation in Ulster. There is no doubt that such parades provoke strife and tension, and such strife and violence on the ground of religious conviction could well be a demonic perversion.

However, this quotation in its actual context comes from a book called GROWING INTO UNION where the authors criticise the Anglican-Methodist Scheme for Reunion on the grounds of institutionalism and uniformity surrounding the 1662 Prayer Book. Why should institutionalism in this connection be considered demonic? It may well be limited, or lacking conviction, but that does not necessarily imply that it is demonic. The strange fact is that when a local Methodist minister was arranging a Holy Communion service with our congregation, he asked that we might have the 1662 service as his people were familiar with it, whereas they would not know the modern series, I or II, used by Anglicans. We seem to forget that in Wesley's Chapel in City Road there lies the 1662 Prayer Book that Wesley used. Far from being a false point of uniformity, the 1662 Prayer Book may well be a true point of unity for Anglicans and Methodists.

However, the tensions that exist in the Churches in England are nothing to be compared with those in Ireland. It is no doubt true that there are political and other factors involved in the strife in Northern Ireland, but fundamentally the tension is between Catholics and Protestants, a matter of religious tradition and conviction which leads to bloodshed in the streets, such as the shooting of a R.C. priest taking the last rites to a dying man. One Belfast Catholic said to me "One man (Christ) died for us all," and this fundamental Christian fact has so often been forgotten in the violence and strife. It is here that the evil of disunity is seen in all its horror, not in schemes for unity, or patterns of uniformity. Cardinal Heenan refers to an occasion when he was to lay the foundation stone of a Cistercian abbey in Northern Ireland, he said,

> "*I told them that being a Christian is more important than being a Catholic or Protestant. I was not intending to enunciate any theological principle but merely to encourage friendship between Christians whose hostility has caused nothing but harm in the history of Ireland. I was surprised at the reaction of some Catholics . . . some well educated Catholics were apparently quite shocked by my words. It is an illusion to think that the average Catholic is yearning to identify himself with his non-Catholic brethren.*"*

I was in Northern Ireland in 1969 when the British troops first entered the streets of Belfast. I saw the broken windows, and roads blocked by paving stones. I preached at a Church near Belfast on the text, "One Lord, one faith, one baptism," and as I talked to some of the people, one of them said "You English do not understand." It is difficult to understand why Christians should fire at one another on the grounds of religious tradition or conviction, unless it is diabolically inspired. It is a curious thing that I have had a few individuals who have flown to see me for exorcism from Belfast, Londonderry and Dublin in the past two years—some Catholics and some Protestants. Each revealed evil which was in some way connected with violence, and desired to be released from the hatred and resentment involved.

It is so sad to see how religious traditions become the cause of strife. Here indeed is a demonic perversion of the Christian truth—'peace on earth, goodwill towards men'. Apart from Ireland, we also have to recognise the demonic powers of evil in a wider context. The Archbishop of York says (quoting Kenneth Slack)

> "*I wondered whether the demonic power of evil was being seen sufficiently clearly—the power that struck down Martin Luther King and held Nigerians and Biafrans in its grip.*"**

* CHRISTIAN UNITY—A CATHOLIC VIEW, Heenan, pp. 1, 2.
** SINEWS OF FAITH, p. 17.

Actually, during the Biafran War, both Biafrans and Nigerians worshipped together in our Universal Prayer Group in Christian fellowship. I have attempted to show in these illustrations, that evil is not essentially found in white sport but in racial discrimination, not in institutional forms or schemes but in religious strife.

Evil and the dead

Now let us consider another sphere which is sometimes considered evil without qualification—what the Bishop of Southwark calls 'psi-phenomena'. Michael Harper says the question the Bishop poses "Can we communicate with the Dead" ought to be "May we communicate with the Dead"* implying that such a practice is forbidden by the Bible. People who regard the bible in this way, refuse to recognise that the bible was not intended to lay down conditions of this kind. After all, Jesus Christ himself communicated with Moses and Elijah in the Holy Mount. Surely the point about communicating with the dead is not whether it should be done, but how it is done. Personally, I am firmly convinced that I saw and spoke to my father after his death in the Church where he had been Vicar during a Communion Service. The Bishop of Southwark mentions in an article to the Times that he communicated with his father after his death.** The Bishop also in this article treated the whole matter of 'psi-phenomena' as a sphere for exploration and research. People may not know that there is a Churches' Fellowship for Psychic and Spiritual Studies. After all why should 'psi-phenomena' or ghosts be considered evil? I am not denying that there are dangers in seances, spiritualism and the use of ouja boards, as I shall show later in this book, but merely pointing out that psychic phenomena can be explored in a detached way without involving moral principle or violating religious conviction.

* Spiritual Warfare, Harper, pp. 47, 48.
** May 3rd, 1969.
See also my letter to the Times, 9th May, 1969.

Exorcism is not eseentially intended to deal with ghosts or even houses, but with the states of soul of living people molested by evil spirits or evil forces. Departed or discarnate spirits often need "requiems" or commendatory prayers for the soul, rather than exorcism. Some priests claim that all spirits are departed, others claim that all are evil and there are no unquiet souls. I am convinced that through vibrations one can discern whether a disturbance is due to an evil spirit or departed spirit or both. An interest in the psychic can lead to a deeper understanding of the spiritual, but can equally well lead to witchcraft. Psychic awareness is a natural gift, like painting or singing. A man may dedicate his gift to God for others or use it for selfish ends. Sometimes people confuse the magical and the mystical because they do not clearly differentiate between the spiritual and the psychic. If exorcism is bible based but not confined to the bible, then it is essentially concerned with people. Jesus cast out demons from people who were possessed or oppressed. Evil comes through people, and only has a secondary or residual effect on places or houses. Places are affected because the people who lived there enacted evil deeds. Jesus was concerned with the souls of men not with buildings.

Exorcism for today

In the popular mind, exorcism is associated with ghosts and the medieval ritual of bell, book and candle. Many people do not seem to associate it with possessed states caused by evil forces. Some people even suggest that evil is in the mind which is a failure to face the fact that evil lies in events and incidents rather than in ideas. During the War of 1939–45 those of us who served in the Forces were under no illusion about the evil of Nazi tyranny. Here was an excellent example of evil for the very symbol of the Nazi Cross—the crooked cross—was a symbol of hatred and violence in complete contrast to Christ's Cross—the symbol of love and peace. Neville Chamberlain was expressing a profound truth when he differentiated between the German people and the Nazi regime. This strange Nazi spirit has influenced people years after the War. One man told me he had picked up the Nazi spirit from visiting the grave of a Nazi airman shot down in England during the war. He even grew a moustache like Hitler, and said he felt as if he were obsessed by a Nazi. I exorcised him and this obsession left him. Another man who had been in a prisoner of war camp in Germany went into strange states where he started speaking German, which he had never learnt, and clenching his fist. When I exorcised him these strange states ceased. Another man was influenced by a strange experience he had when he entered a German tank to find the Nazi soldiers dead. Although he had had psychiatric treatment, this experience remained and it was only after exorcism that it dissolved from his memory. Another young man became "obsessed" by Nazi spirit by visiting Germany after which he acquired an obsession for Nazi ideals, but this led him near to self-destruction. After I had exorcised him, he produced suicide letters.

One of the strangest experiences I have had was the exorcism of a yacht which belonged to the Nazis and was captured by the British at the end of the 1939–45 War. The owner was convinced that the Nazis had put a kind of curse on it as certain fatal and strange accidents occurred in connection with the yacht over a number of years. When I exorcised the yacht the owner felt a departed spirit leave him and I heard a voice shouting German which suddenly ceased. Clearly the Nazi influence had disappeared.

Why today?

I give these illustrations to show the influence of evil which cannot be denied by those who experienced it through the 1939–45 War. It is a known fact that the Nazi leaders used occult forces to aid their violence and destruction.* Archbishop Temple expressed the Nazi spirit when he said "it was not doing evil knowing that it was wrong but believing that it was right". In

* Man, Myth and Magic, No. 69 (National Socialism).

another context completely today the same outlook has affected the 'permissive society', where people claim that certain precepts like the ten commandments are outmoded, and so such a conception of society opens the way to evil,—violence or illicit sex. The underlying problem of the possessed or oppressed is moral not psychic. The power of Satan over souls is through moral evil. A man who came to me about manifestations in his house once said, "Why should such things happen to innocent people?" I simply told him to examine himself to see whether he was so innocent. It then transpired that he had had an illicit affair, and his wife had done shoplifting, and neither were innocent. A man came to me saying he had been disturbed by a woman's voice during a seance; it transpired that he was having an affair without his family's knowledge. A woman said she had had a male spirit visit her at night; this referred to the memory of another man friend apart from marriage. A couple said there were disturbances in the house at night; they were living together having each left their own married partner.

Evil and sin

It is not often recognised that the Common Law of this country is based on the ten commandments. To ignore this is to do so at one's peril; it may even 'court disaster' or at least lead to a good deal of unhappiness. At the same time many people today approach relationships not from the point of view of law but of love. There is a I believe a greater sensitiveness to other people's needs and in consequence a recognition of hurting others through cruel actions or through unfulfilled affairs. A sense of guilt seems to come more through the break up of an affair or through the hurt involved, rather than during the affair or in the doing of a violent act. People appear to be not so concerned about breaking the law as violating another person's personality.

We seem to forget the role of the devil as an accuser. The devil has always picked on illicit relationships or violent actions to torment the soul and now has an easy opportunity through the permissive society. It is often through awareness of evil rather than consciousness of sin that people turn to God. Exorcism is not a form of white magic to release evil. It involves a personal confrontation with the person and a recognition of wrong—or sin if you like—in order that the evil forces may be released.

The task of the Church

The task of the Church is the cure of souls, and not to be deflected into psychic sidetracks, or become too involved in social or political issues. A general, who is a keen Christian, recently said to me that was a very great pity that clergy so often spoke on political and social issues, but appeared to say very little on spiritual issues at a time when many young people and others were seeking for spiritual things, often outside the Church. There is a tendency today to look for evil in social and political issues in a corporate sense, instead of taking a more radical view, and recognising it in the souls of men. It is well to remember that "deliver us from evil" in the Lord's prayer might well be said corporately, but it is also said by countless millions in their private prayers.

CHAPTER 2

DELIVER US FROM EVIL—LIBERATION

Exorcism is sometimes called 'deliverance', and rightly so because it is not purely a negative thing, a removal of evil forces or spirits, but a liberation, giving the person not purely freedom from evil but freedom for service to God and man. There is a danger of regarding exorcism like magic in the sense that one exorcism will alter the person, but this is frequently not the case. For deliverance or liberation a person sometimes needs a number of exorcisms. One exorcism sometimes uncovers the need for another because it brings to consciousness other evil forces or influences. Often people who request exorcism expect too much too soon, and do not recognise that a lot depends upon their co-operation and their willingness to surrender to God anything which obstructs their liberation from evil. It is useful to differentiate between major and minor exorcisms. Major exorcisms involve dealing with people who are actually possessed or oppressed by an evil force or spirit, and would normally require a priest trained and experienced in exorcism. Minor exorcisms refer to an evil influence or force infesting or infecting a person through being involved in an activity like ouja boards, or through association with a person who is possessed. Major exorcisms and minor exorcisms can well be compared to major and minor operations. Major exorcisms, like major operations, should be done by the specialist, the priest who is knowledgeable and experienced in such matters. Minor exorcisms can be done by any priest in the course of pastoral duties.

Libera nos

The prayer in the missal which follows the Lord's Prayer is:

> "*Deliver us (Libera nos) from all evil past present and to come that by thine availing mercy, we may be liberated from all sin and safe from all distress.*"

It expresseses the whole idea of 'liberation' beautifully. Exorcism liberates a person from the grips of evil torment but it does not take away temptation which often recurs. The significant difference is often recognised sometime afterwards, may be some weeks or months, not sometimes in the way the person expects but in an unexpected way when he is not looking for it. He seems to find a new liberation, a freedom *not* to sin, as St. Augustine called it. St. Augustine differentiated between a freedom to sin which he called licence, and a freedom not to sin which he called liberty. It should be remembered that conditions of life in his day were not so different from our own with a permissive society. Twenty or thirty years ago, salvation was the word emphasised by Evangelistic Campaigns or Missions which, with notable exceptions like the Billy Graham Crusade, seem to have lost some of their impact. Today in many spheres of life the word liberation has become a key word. We hear of the Women's Liberation movement, the Gay Liberation movement and many others. Liberation from evil has far more significance of meaning nowadays than salvation from sin, largely because the consciousness of sin has waned, but the awareness of evil has increased. People who are not necessarily religious and would not use the word sin at all, are nevertheless aware of evil, and it is sometimes at this point that they turn to God through fear of evil. Here is a wonderful opportunity for the Church to meet a spiritual need, and Harvey Cox may well be right when he says the function of the Church in the modern age should be that of cultural exorcism.

The cultural exorcist

Harvey Cox, in SECULAR CITY, states:

> *"Though it frequently embarrasses us today, Jesus was viewed by his own age as a great exorcist. His power to cast out demons was central to his ministry. It focused all his various roles. As one who announced the New Age, he commanded the evil spirits to depart . . . As healer and reconciler, he exorcised them to restore people to their places in the community . . . All of this sounds extremely peculiar to modern ears. Most of us would prefer to forget that for many of his contemporaries Jesus' exorcism was in no way peripheral, but stood at the heart of his work. How does the Church carry on this function today?"**

Harvey Cox makes the very important point that exorcism was central to Jesus' ministry. He goes on to say:

> *"Jesus dealt in his exorcism with individuals, but his whole life represented a kind of sweeping exorcism of a whole culture. He confronted demonic images and legalistic compulsions in such a way that people were* liberated *from both into clearheaded and productive ways of life . . . Confronting people with what is really there is always a painful process . . . It was what Jesus was always doing and it represents an indispensable element of the church's function in the secular city."**

Exorcism—a confrontation

I am fully aware that Harvey Cox refers to the exorcism of a culture in a corporate sense, but in linking it to Jesus' exorcism of individuals he shows the relevance of exorcism to individuals as well. If we regard exorcism in this sort of way, we will see it has a very important function in our secular age. Far from being out of date, it is very much up to date. Instead of being regarded as a rather odd interest of a few priests and others interested in ghosts, it should be seen as a function central to the ministry. Exorcism is a form of personal confrontation—this is a wonderful

* THE SECULAR CITY, Harvey Cox, p. 161, 168.

description of what happens in the spiritual interview when in a moment of truth a person faces his life and recognises his fears and failures in relation to God. Exorcism of individuals can act as a transforming influence in society. This exposing of evil sometimes produces physical manifestations such as a cold shiver or strange convulsive movements, or a sudden burst into tears, in men and those not easily moved to tears. It is almost as important, or perhaps in some cases more important, than the laying on of hands and prayers. Sometimes people have said they felt different before they have been into church for any rite purely through confrontation with what is really there, as Harvey Cox put it. Harvey Cox does not refer to the rite of exorcism, but the principle behind exorcism which he links to the exorcisms of Jesus himself. It is often asserted that Jesus cast out devils at a distance in the case of the Syro Phoenician woman's daughter,* and on first consideration it appears to be the case. However, we should further consider this in relation to its parallel, the Canaanitish woman.** Both the New English Bible and Jerusalem Bible describe her condition as tormented by a devil. It is described as a healing rather than a casting out. It is perhaps a relief from torment rather than a release from bondage. This seems to me to be the most likely explanation as in all the other instances of diabolical molestation, Jesus personally confronted the individual. I am convinced that essentially exorcism involves personal confrontation. At the same time, an exorcism prayer can be used for relief but personal confrontation is essential for release. For instance, an American rang me up from New York and I said a prayer over the telephone which he admitted gave him relief, but he still needed to fly to London for exorcism to receive full release. I have often been asked by people from the U.S.A., Australia and other parts of the world whether I could exorcise them without meeting them. I have had to explain that exorcism, unlike healing, cannot be done at a distance but only through

* Mark 7, 26–30.
** Matthew 15, 21–28.

personal confrontation. Occasionally, one finds that after an exorcism, the person rings up to say the devil or demon is still there. The real interpretation is that they are tormented by the devil but no longer possessed or oppressed. An exorcism prayer over the telephone or otherwise at that time may cause the torment to cease. Torment is due to past experiences occasionally occurring in dreams, and at other times.

Church—The natural place

People sometimes say, "Is it necessary to go into a Church?" I find in fact that people will go into church for exorcism who do not normally go to church. Some have no connection whatever with it, and there are some even who belong to other religions. Jews, Moslems and Hindus who will do so. It seems natural to them that the church should be used for exorcism without qualm or quibble. Although two witches started by saying they would not enter the church, they ultimately both did so for exorcism. After all the church has the natural atmosphere of prayer and therefore is the most effective place, but it is not necessary to do an exorcism in a church. When I exorcise houses, it is my normal practice to exorcise or bless the people in the house because often it is one or more of the people who are affecting the condition of the house. Sometimes people ask me to perform the rite of exorcism or conduct a service of exorcism, but both these phrases are inadequate and reflect an attitude towards exorcism which is pietistic rather than practical. It is often suggested by people that exorcism helps those who are conditioned by belief in demons by satisfying their supposed need but this is a travesty of the truth.

An actual force

Exorcism is the removal of an actual force which can be felt by impartial observers, and is in no way intended to palliate neurotic people who imagine they are possessed. For instance there were two separate occasions when observers, a photographer and a reporter had come to attend exorcisms for professional reasons.

They were each personally affected by the exorcisms they saw, and each asked for exorcisms for themselves. The reporter said he felt a force shoot at him from the man being exorcised who oddly enough asserted that nothing had happened. The photographer said the force was so strong he could not hold his camera straight. Both these men were taken unawares by an objective force which neither was expecting. In fact the reporter later told me that he came to see the exorcism as a sceptical agnostic, but as he left the church he had reluctantly to acknowledge that what he witnessed was in fact true.

The method of exorcism

In the Old Testament and among the Jews, exorcism was carried out by incantations. From the early traditions of the Church a form of exorcism had been inserted into the baptism rite and so became essentially ritualistic. There is actually a form of exorcism in the Baptism service in the 1549 Prayer Book. In the Roman Catholic Church there is an order of exorcists, one of the minor orders, and so it is essentially a rite, whilst in the Orthodox Church it appears to have been used by monks with special gifts authorised to do it. As we see it in Jesus himself, it was not essentially ritualistic at all; it differed from the Jews and was essentially a word of command combined with a divine touch. Some exorcists say you should not lay hands on a possessed person, but they seem to forget that Jesus laid his hands on the woman whom Satan had bound and loosed her from a spirit of infirmity. I am convinced that some are not loosed because this element has been ignored. "If I by the finger of God, cast out devils,"* it was for Jesus confrontation with an individual in a concrete situation. He commanded the demon to depart and cast it forth through his hands. Both command and touch are essential elements in it. Some priests emphasise the correct formula, others the need of a praying group, but neither of these are essential. It is not the rite

* Lu. 13: 11–16 and Lu. 11 : 20.

nor the group that makes the exorcism, but the Holy Spirit mediated through the words and actions of the exorcist. As Ling points out:

> "*The essential point in Jesus's claim is that his exorcisms are the work of the Spirit of God. The only exorcism that is likely to be lasting is that which is the work of the Holy Spirit.*"*

The formula not important

We cannot quench the spirit of God by insisting on a particular ritualistic formula with incense or holy water, nor a particular kind of group prayer meeting with extensive prayers lasting for hours. If we look more deeply into Jesus's own method we see it was simple and immediate, and met the situation as it arose, but essentially practical and not pietistic. The great difference between the exorcist in our day and Jesus is not in the method but in fact that Jesus "knew what was in man," whilst the exorcist today needs to interview the person for an hour or more to uncover and expose the evil. Some exorcists seem to consider that all that is needed is to use a certain formula to anyone who appears to think they are possessed regardless of diagnosis. This seems to assume that some who are disturbed might think they are possessed. From experience of hundreds of people, I find that the majority of those who request exorcism are aware, sometimes rather reluctantly, of evil molestation, and the diagnosis confirms their own awareness. It often gives them intense relief to be told that what they suspected is accurate. They then explain that doctors and priests have frequently misunderstood what they said. As Ling points out:

> "*If exorcism is not the positive work of the Holy Spirit driving out and replacing the power of the demon, the result will be worse than the original condition.*"**

* SIGNIFICANCE OF SATAN, p. 19.
** SIGNIFICANCE OF SATAN, p. 21.

A psychiatrist once sent me a man who had only two days before seen another exorcist who used a formula in this way. The man had suicidal thoughts a few hours afterwards because no deep diagnosis had been made. I have had numerous requests from people who have been to parish priests or others who have purely said prayers or used a particular ritual without any effect whatsoever, and yet I found after confrontation in an interview, the evil dissolved. For instance, a priest wrote to me telling me how a man came to him saying he had a curse put on him by a man whom he had sacked at work. This priest exorcised him four times, but although he felt a relief he did not get release. At the request of the priest, I saw the man and challenged him about the incident, and the evil was exposed when the man admitted having an affair with a relative of the man he had sacked. That is why the curse worked, and immediately this was exposed the effects of the curse lifted. Now, I do not mean that there cannot be an immediate awareness which discerns the problem, and acts on it on some occasions, but often it requires a prolonged interview. Actually two different priests told me of incidents which made them use an exorcism although neither had ever done so before. Each of them was faced with a man who showed signs of evil possession and each used some immediate word of command in the name of Christ and the evil immediately dissolved. The formula or form did not matter; it was the action which I firmly believe was the action of the Holy Spirit. Each of these priests through the experience has since explored the matter of exorcism in depth. Like baptism, anyone can exorcise in an emergency, and I have known laymen and laywomen do so with effect, but it is obviously better that a trained priest should do so normally as an exorcism can have a reaction on the person who does it unless they are orientated to it. I have had to explain sometimes to bishops that circumstances sometimes require immediate action, and cannot be arranged like a marriage, otherwise the person might try suicide. Naturally bishops who are spiritually and pastorally minded recognise this. There was one occasion when a girl who had been sent to me by a psychiatrist attended a confirmation with two friends. She had attempted to jump out of the car whilst on their way. I exorcised her immediately with the Bishop present who gave her a blessing afterwards.

It can return

Ling draws attention to the fact that the teaching of Jesus illuminated for his contemporaries a fact of which they were already aware that those who had been exorcised did become re-possessed. Every exorcist must realise that this is always a possibility, not necessarily through the fault of the person exorcised, although this is sometimes the case, but through his misfortune. For instance, a young man told me of an incident of violence he had witnessed by another young man. After the evil fear had been exorcised, he unexpectedly met the man again and the evil force returned. It should be recognised that each exorcism should clear the force of evil but it may return. It only remains at the time if the person holds on to the evil through fear or doubt and refuses to surrender to God in faith. Every exorcism is a purging of spiritual defilement and the teaching of Jesus reiterates this fact by his emphasis on the unclean spirit, a phrase used frequently in the Gospels.

"Unclean spirit"

The phrase 'unclean spirit' is a remarkable description of some of the conditions we find in people today. The African group, to which I have already referred, have what they call a cleansing ceremony on the first Sunday of every month when the sign of the cross is used with holy water to cleanse them from evil spirits. The ceremony is the same whether the members are Roman Catholics, Anglicans or Free Church and accepted as such, it is something which expresses a far deeper significance than mere ritual. People who request exorcism often say they feel unclean—sometimes through strange sex perversions or even drug addicts.

People who have contracted habits rightly considered filthy are excellent examples of the compelling force of an unclean spirit.

Naturally, uncleanness is often associated with sex and one of the worst forms is that of incest. A girl once told me that because she had been the victim of incestuous intercourse with her father, she found all idea of sex unclean and any relationship with a young man was repugnant. Another young woman said her marriage was unhappy because of an assault made upon her by a man when she was a young teenager. A young student told me how his whole life had been affected by a priest who had abused him homosexually. In each of these cases, an unclean spirit had remained with the person through their unpleasant experience distorting their whole outlook on sex. They were each spiritually defiled, and needed the cleansing of exorcism.

The dirty old man syndrome

Far from being outmoded the term 'unclean spirit' is quite extraordinarily relevant to certain conditions today. I have known hundreds of people who have suffered from sensations which make them feel unclean even to the extent of embarrassment in the company of others. Many have consulted psychiatrists entirely without effect because such a condition relates to past incidents or sins where kinky sex was involved. One young man came on numerous occasions for exorcism without release until he openly admitted a weird form of oral sex which had given him a form of self-disgust. Once this was exposed, he was liberated. The danger of the permissive society is that it tends to give the impression that it no longer matters what form of sex is used. Actually young people could not be more deceived because so often certain types of 'kinky sex' twist the personality of a person to such an extent that he or she no longer desires the normal. One of the difficulties with homosexuality which is not often recognised is the fact that one of the partners who is homosexual may twist the other who is not that way inclined until he imagines that he could be. A sensitive person can sometimes perceive the twisted sex of another and be affected by it. When people used to speak of a 'dirty old man'—such a phrase well expresses what is meant by an unclean spirit. Masturbation when it is combined with self excitation through sex fantasies can have a devastating effect on the personality. The attempt by certain psychiatrists to belittle this practice as unimportant is singularly unconvincing. One middle-aged man who had been to psychiatrists and priests for twenty years told me that this practice had nearly driven him to attempt suicide because of the distortion of his whole soul through it. He was immensely relieved that it was taken seriously by me and found quite a new release through exorcism. The fact is that masturbation relates to sex incidents which have occurred with others and is not normally due to imaginations conjured up for satisfaction which is often too glibly assumed by priests or psychiatrists who have not taken the trouble to find the cause or the circumstances in which the habit started.

Sex—A moral issue

Many people are coming to recognise that certain sex fantasies are not necessarily mental aberrations to be treated by medical means but moral issues to be faced without any attempt to hide or deceive and cleansed by absolution and exorcism. Certain types of sensation are psychic essentially not psychological and need the sword of the spirit to cut the psychic links with the past. People suffering from this kind of unclean spirit must be completely open and not try to disguise the facts. Self deception or self protection postpones release.

People do not often realise that the permissive society opens the way to demonic seductive forces. Numerous young girls have told me how they have been seduced at a young age and subsequently found sex repellent. Psychiatrists may discover the cause but cannot remove the seductive force. One girl only recently said how she felt cleansed by exorcism. The seductive force grips the unconscious and inhibits normal sex relations but exorcism liberates the person and opens the way to a new love. Seduction is not just loose sex but the deliberate violation of the sacredness of the personality—the invasion of the inmost soul. I know one model who had been seduced by her agent without having any real sex at all. She came to see me because she felt she had lost her soul to him, not purely her body.

In the same way, young men are often inhibited in sex relations with girls because they have been seduced at a young age homosexually. A young man broke away from an older man who had been a homosexual partner not purely because of sex but because he would lose his soul to him.

The Gadarene Question

Jesus also exorcised those described as "possessed . . . exceeding fierce." Clearly people who had violent spirits because "no man might pass by that way." Violence was clearly a symptom of the possessed. Now Michael Harper rather strangely asserts that the Gadarene demoniac was mentally deranged but I consider that this is an inadequate presentation of the facts. A doctor once pointed out to me that in his opinion there were two kinds of schizophrenics. One kind of schizophrenic is the person who has a chemical infection of the brain and his condition is medical—the other is the person who is possessed by an evil spirit or force and his condition is spiritual. Therefore I submit that the Gadarene demoniac is a spiritual schizophrenic, not mentally deranged but demonically motivated.*

Doctor or exorcist?

At the same time, there might well be some patients in mental hospitals who are possessed but considered mentally deranged because no one has diagnosed their possession. Recently I received an unusual request from a consultant psychiatrist, a very perceptive doctor who told me of a patient of his who had been treated in a number of other hospitals by medical means without

* Matt. 8: 28; see also Mark 5: 15.

effect and he was of the opinion that he might be possessed. It was arranged that I should exorcise him in the hospital chapel with the psychiatrist present as he had not normally been allowed out of the hospital because he had been violent in a number of ways. The psychiatrist later told me that the patient had become a changed man who was later able to live at home as an out patient. Incidentally, this same doctor asked me to see another patient of his who claimed to be possessed. However, we both agreed that he appeared to be a medical schizophrenic.

Hells Angels

One of the most frightening experiences I have had was when the Chaplain of a prison asked me to come and exorcise two Hell's Angels in the Prison Chapel. Here there was clearly no doubt about the violence, one had been sentenced for malicious wounding with a knife and the other with holding a gun with intent to harm. The strangest thing about it was why they asked to be exorcised. They explained that they had been connected with black magic and had dedicated themselves to the devil to harm others. They had now become afraid that when they left the prison they might murder someone and would not be able to control themselves. They were almost afraid to go into the Chapel because of their former connection with black magic. The first man went out into unconsciousness under the exorcism and was brought round with holy water. The second man went dazed and later came round. Eventually when they had recovered their equilibrium they said they had lost all fear of the Chapel and asked for a bible. A Franciscan brother who had attended them produced a bible and we read Mark 5 about the violent men. They then said it spoke to their condition and asked questions about the Church. They had clearly been 'possessed'.

Another case of Hell's Angels was that of a young man in Borstal, imprisoned for participating in gang violence. In this case I was asked to exorcise him with the psychiatrist and the probation officer present. Both the psychiatrist and the probation officer said that they were shattered by the experience and recognised the tremendous power of the evil force that possessed him but never for one moment questioned the need for exorcism. The young man was cleared.

Another case was one of a young man who was permitted by a Roman Catholic psychiatrist to be brought out of a mental hospital accompanied by a male nurse for exorcism. He had tried to strangle his mother with a strange violence but it subsided after the exorcism and he was later able to be rehabilitated. Both these men showed similar symptoms of violence to the demoniacs in the Gospels and reveal the relevance of possession as mentioned in the Gospels to our modern life today.

Possession still with us

In contrast, Michael Harper asserts that no true Christian can be taken over as the word possession suggests. He also claims that possession is not a Bible word and tries to translate δαιμονιηοζαι as "having a spirit" rather than "to be possessed". Actually John Robinson, an eminent New Testament scholar, pointed out to me that δαιμονιηυζαι does in fact mean to be possessed and he could not see how it could mean anything else. In any case there is a clear distinction made in the New Testament between δαιμονιηοζαι (to be possessed) and δαιμονιον εχειν, (to have a spirit*) which is actually used in reference to Jesus himself. All the new translations translate δαιμονιηοζαι as 'possessed'.

It is assumed that possessed means demon possessed, but it is valuable to consider the deeper meaning of the word demon. δαιμων in Classical Greek meant a deity, but was translated as demon in New Testament Greek. Actually the Classical Greek gives a shade of meaning which sheds new light because it shows that to be 'demon possessed' is to be 'spellbound'—bound to a deity like the ancient classical gods. For instance when Billy Graham said "The people of England have gone after other gods—

* Jo. 10: 20. N.S.V., N.E.B. and Jerusalem Bible.

the god of sex, the god of money . . .," surely it was in this sense that people can become demon possessed. For instance some are bound to Venus—the goddess of sex, or Bacchus—the god of wine, or Pan, who now seems to have become the god of drugs. Actually, Canon Pearce Higgins says he has never come across a demon in investigating cases of possession, but he is looking for it in old categories. If it is to be seen in modern ways, I submit that it is in being spellbound to a deity or false god which will make demon possession meaningful. Now, I am not suggesting that every nymphomaniac, drunkard or drug addict is possessed, that is arrant nonsense. What I am saying is that when a man or woman becomes drawn to kinky sex, heavy drinking or drugs they open themselves to evil forces which sometimes take over and possess them through the opening they have made. As St. Augustine once said, 'a habit not resisted becomes a necessity'. Here is the slavery to Satan and his demons, or deities if you like, from which liberation is needed.

Not devils but spirits

At the same time, there is sometimes a multiple possession not only by demons or deities but through overshadowing by discarnate human spirits. Canon Pearce Higgins mentions 114 out of 400 cases of mental illness being due to possession by discarnate human spirits. Overshadowing as well as possession is a New Testament word. The Virgin Mary was 'overshadowed' by the Holy Ghost. We often hear of a person being overshadowed by someone and we have found people who have been overshadowed by their near relatives who have recently died. Often the person who is overshadowed acquires the habits which the discarnate spirit had in his earthly life. For instance a man is overshadowed by his late grandfather, who was a drunkard, another man is overshadowed by his late brother who was violent. However, in each case there was also a demon behind. The discarnate spirit could be drawn away but the demon still needed to be cast out.

Christians not exempt

Apart from the New Testament, contemporary cultured people, whether religious or not, often use the word 'possessed' whereas 'having a spirit', unless of course it was an overshadowing, would have no real significance of meaning for them.

Actually, Michael Harper seems to be under some misapprehension about what a true Christian can experience regarding possession. There was a dedicated, Christian worker who was 'bewitched' (or possessed) by a witch she tried to help. She never lost her devotion and was cleared by exorcism. The criterion of a true Christian is devotion not experience.*

Someone at a conference said he could not see how a person who was possessed could receive communion. He did not realise that some people who are possessed are not fully conscious of it and would purely follow their normal practice. For instance, I have known two priests, both celebrating communion regularly, who had become possessed. Both priests had a real vocation and had done excellent spiritual work for God as I believe Judas did. Both seemed gripped by a growing moral deterioration. In one case, it started with a wrong relationship with a girl and in the other a wrong relationship with a young man. In each case, the relationship had caused their prayer life and living contact with God to disappear and both gradually developed a kind of double deception—an apparent holiness on the one hand and a secret wickedness on the other. Their consciences became dulled and their sensitivity hardened. Their actions were diabolically clever, their judgements clouded and the demonic grip widened over different areas of life—family and sex relationships and money matters became twisted. Like the possessed man in the Gospels there were a 'legion of devils'. Exorcism gave each of them an awareness of the evil which had been happening and touched the spring of desire to be different. Each in their own way

* Spiritual Warfare. Harper, pp. 109, 110.

found a renewal of the spiritual life and a revival of their priesthood and ministry.

Many forms of possession

One of the strangest cases of possession was that of a former Salvation Army Officer married to a Salvation Army lass. His wife died whilst he was serving in the Forces and he suddenly changed. He posed as a bachelor with a homosexual friend, acted under an assumed name and started speaking a language he had never learned. After exorcisms over a period when the deception was exposed, he remarried and started an entirely new life. Possession takes many forms and it is not easily discernible, but in each case the person is taken over by an external evil force —but only because he has allowed his will to pursue evil.

Possession may be due in some cases to a person consciously giving themselves to the devil in a clear and definite form, as in witchcraft. In others it may be due to having drifted into evil ways to such an extent that they become alien to Christian precepts and principles. One man said he had made a compact with the devil. A girl said she had been married to the devil and became a witch. They both knew they were possessed because they had consciously willed it. The difficulty of diagnosis arises where people are largely unaware of possession yet know in their inmost soul that they have no peace, however much they deceive themselves.

I cannot understand why the recent Exorcism report says the concept of possession is dubious.* It is very much a feature of our modern life. The possessed is not owned by the demon but temporarily taken over until exorcism dispels it.

Oppression and possession

It is not easy to perceive possession in people because they are diabolically clever and easily deceive people who are unaccustomed to discern their condition. The reason for this is that the

* Exorcism Report, p. 23.

evil force or demon controls their unconscious and only manifests itself occasionally in such moments when they become virulent or violent. People often say after exorcism that they did not feel anything which is due to the fact that the evil force grips the unconscious. People often describe someone as possessed who would be better described as oppressed. 'Discernment' of spirits is needed to diagnose the difference. The 'oppressed' are not controlled by a demon but distorted. They are more aware of what is happening and have a measure of freedom which is not found in the "possessed". This phrase is also used in the New Testament in reference to Jesus' exorcisms: "Jesus . . . went about doing good and healing all that were oppressed of the devil."* This condition of oppression, in contrast to possession which is comparatively rare, is found fairly frequently. I think it far better describes what happens to a person than the word obsession which has psychological overtones. Oppression describes this rather strange force that attaches itself to a person without gripping them completely. They become conscious of a weight interfering with their actions but not controlling them. We find this sort of Satanic oppression in the Gospels, playing on an emotion like fear, doubt or hate.

St. Peter oppressed

Take for example Jesus dealing with his own disciples. Peter, for instance, appears oppressed by a demonic fear, he fails to do the right thing because he is afraid of doing the wrong thing. Hence we find him saying to Jesus "Be it far from thee Lord" and Jesus saying to Peter "Get thee behind me, Satan."** We find the same attitude in his denial but "the Lord turned and looked upon Peter"†—he confronted him and Peter wept. The haunting fear

* Acts 10: 38.
** Math. 16: 22, 23.
† Math. 26: 69–76.

changed to boldness and an adventurous spirit after the Resurrection.

I remember well a young theological student coming to me at the suggestion of another because he was afraid to go forward to ordination. I exorcised him of his spirit of fear and he was ordained. Some years later he had the same fear on the brink of marriage. I exorcised him again and he went ahead. The diabolical attack was against vocation, but now he is a splendid priest, husband and father. This fear was an oppressive force, a tormenting fear which made him nearly fail to do the right thing through fear of doing the wrong thing.

The Thomas syndrome

Take another instance, Thomas was oppressed by an overwhelming sense of doubt. Like many agnostics of modern times he could say "we know not whither thou goest, how can we know the way".* This was a spiritual condition, not purely an intellectual one, a failure to understand and follow a way of life due to uncertainty more than a lack of intellectual conviction. He must have evidence of the resurrection, but the converting conviction was the touch of his pierced hands, "Reach hither thy finger and behold my hands," a personal confrontation with the risen Lord.

Now I remember some twenty years ago, a young man who had doubts about the Christian Gospel because of his way of life. Although he had been brought up in a missionary school, he would not enter a church. One day I suggested that he might come to the blessing of an engagement ring of a friend of his and he complied for social reasons. Whilst he was in the church praying I exorcised him and although he was furious at the time he admitted that it was a turning point. He was reconciled to the Church and later became a priest, ordained on St. Thomas's day, but after some years in the ministry he began to doubt his vocation

* Jo. 20: 24–29.

and particularly he doubted the validity of the ministry of healing and exorcism. Jesus revealed to him a hidden power in his hands and this experience reorientated his whole ministry with a new gift of the Holy Spirit because he was no longer faithless but believing. He had felt the touch of Jesus for himself.

The case of Judas

Another obvious example is of course Judas. In popular thought, he is always associated with betrayal, but people so easily forget his excellent work with the other disciples in the early part of Jesus' ministry. Then the devil put into the heart of Judas to betray him, then Satan entered into him. Here we see how an oppression ended in possession and Judas was no longer the victim of Satanic attack but an agent of the evil powers of destruction. In the case of Judas possession took the form of moral deterioration and hate led to betrayal.

I knew a mission preacher who had at one time a passion for souls combined with a golden thread of oratory. He had attracted numbers of people, many in great poverty, in the old days and won them for Christ with great power. There was no doubt about his deep conviction and his concern for others. Unfortunately, a gradual moral deterioration overcame him and his wife left him. Love turned to hate and he recognised the evil forces and requested exorcism. After he was exorcised, he preached again, regaining his former evangelistic zeal, but sadly it did not last. He became involved with a woman and mixed up in his financial affairs. Feeling no doubt that he had betrayed his Lord, like Judas he went out and hanged himself. When I heard the sad news I naturally reproached myself for not being able to help. I had to accept the fact that if Jesus did not stop Judas, we must also be prepared to recognise that there are some people we are not meant to help. People sometimes condemn suicides but forget that one of Jesus' own disciples committed suicide.

What of the other disciples, they all forsook him and fled in the Garden of Gethsemane.

Conversion no protection

There is a strange trait in human nature which makes people flee from a difficult situation. Sometimes the devil by subtle suggestions ensnares them away. I have had the strange and unexpected experience on two separate occasions of finding a priest on my doorstep who had fled from his parish. One had given way to despair, the other had given way to a violent fury. On each occasion I had a desperate wife on the telephone, hoping her husband might come to me and pleading with me for help. Providentially, I was in on both occasions and by the grace of God, each was gently persuaded to come into church for exorcism. In each case, the priest concerned got in his car without another word after the exorcism and returned to his parish. These were further examples of 'Satanic oppression'.

No doubt, I might well be asked why I have given examples of priests and a mission preacher. Once a person said to Archbishop Temple "The clergy are a poor lot" to which he replied "We only have the laity to choose from." That is the point; these stories are stories of ordinary men called to serve God, who were attacked and oppressed by evil forces.

It is quite naive to suggest, as is sometimes suggested, that when a man is converted he is not diabolically attacked. This is quite untrue to the Bible, where Jesus' own disciples were molested by the devil and even Jesus himself was, in the wilderness.

The Magdalene complex

Take another instance from the Gospels, that of Mary Magdalene, one out of whom went seven devils. Here clearly was a girl who had lived a loose sex life, like many today, and yet was transformed by Jesus. A girl once came to see me for exorcism who had tried her vocation as a nun and had later married. It transpired that she had an affair before entering the convent where she had the most horrible sexual torment. The religious atmosphere made it worse and she found no relief in marriage either. Through confession and exorcism this sex oppression was cleansed and she found a new life of peace and joy, like Mary Magdalene after the devils had been cast out. In the same way, a man requested exorcism who had been a lay brother in a monastery and left it. He had violent sex sensations whilst in the monastery and desire for the world. He reminded me of the young man who lacked detachment, one thing thou lackest.* He acknowledged that there had been homosexual incidents before entering the monastic life. He had also found it difficult to adjust to a life of poverty through lack of detachment. After confession and exorcism he found a new peace.

Tempted or tormented

Now I have deliberately taken these examples of two people who were living what is technically known as the 'religious life' because, far from being immune, they were violently tormented by sex sensations which had such a strong grip that not even the regular discipline of Mass, offices, confession and enclosure could quell their power. I think it is important to differentiate between 'torment' and 'temptation'. Temptation is the universal experience of mankind; even Jesus himself was tempted in the wilderness. Torment on the other hand is due to past sins or weaknesses—a demonic attack on a particular emotion. The person needs the ministry of exorcism and often absolution as well. The power to absolve is the power to command the devil to withdraw. "Our Lord Jesus Christ hath left power on earth" as it says in the words of the Absolution in the Anglican Prayer Book. The person tormented must face openly any sins without any attempt to hide or deceive or the torment may remain. Sometimes a person needs 'healing of the memories' because it is a memory, not a recent event, which torments them.

Many people who have come to me for exorcism have themselves used the word 'oppression' without any suggestion from me. Such a word naturally comes to their minds because it

* Mark 10: 21.

expresses an invisible force weighing on their mind and heart and distorting and disturbing their soul. It may come through their own sin or through the sin of another, but it does not seem to disappear of itself.

Guilt oppression

A young airman once told me that he felt an evil oppression due to an incident which occurred in childhood. He happened to knock into his mother when she was carrying his sister, who died shortly after childbirth. He was wrongly accused of killing her, but the medical evidence exonerated him completely. A young married woman told me that she had a haunting sense of guilt from an incident when she put a pillow over a child to stop noise and some weeks afterwards the child died. The medical evidence showed that this incident could not have caused the death, but she felt accused of it. These are excellent examples where false accusations left a scar, in each case for many years. Each felt an evil oppression of guilt, not due to their own actions which were largely innocent, but due to the slanderous words of others.

Afflictions

Affliction* is another word used in the Bible and also commonly used of certain physical conditions now sometimes attributed to psychosomatic causes. Take for example epilepsy. Now it is important to point out that there are two kinds of epilepsy—one that is due to a congenital condition of the brain and another, sometimes called idiopathic epilepsy, which is due to underlying emotional causes. The Greeks even believed that epilepsy was the invasion of the personality by an outside force. Far from being an old-fashioned attitude, it expresses a fundamental truth. Sometimes a distinction is drawn between true and false epilepsy. I have carefully investigated in cases of epilepsy whether there

* Acts 5: 16 afflicted by unclean spirits.

has been an encephalograph and if the brain is affected then it should be treated medically. If, on the other hand, the brain has not been affected, then it could well be false or idiopathic epilepsy and may be due to demonic forces.

Epileptic affliction

A striking example of this kind of condition in the New Testament is what is sometimes called the epileptic boy.* One day, a man came to see me and whilst he was talking to me, he started making convulsive movements and lost control. I immediately rebuked the unclean spirit and he became completely calm. He then looked out of the window and said he saw the shadow of his former self and could laugh at it. I subsequently investigated his background and discovered that the doctors had described his condition as idiopathic epilepsy. These fits began after he left his wife and went off with another woman, the unclean spirit had gripped him. He was subsequently anointed and found new peace.

A woman was brought by her husband who had fits from early childhood. An encephalograph had been taken and there was no infection of the brain. Whilst she was talking to me, she started convulsive movements and I immediately exorcised her before we had time to go to church. We traced the fits back to an incestuous assault on her by her brother when she was a small girl. Again, there was an unclean spirit which invaded her and had to be released. She was later confirmed and found new spiritual strength.

Affliction—Physical condition

An 'affliction' in contrast to possession or oppression is a physical condition due to demonic forces. Another example in the New Testament is the woman who was bound by Satan for eighteen years. Now I was once asked to see a woman whose legs

* Luke 9: 37.

had been paralysed for fifteen years and the doctors claimed that there was no medical cause. It transpired that fifteen years before, her husband had left her for another woman. She had tried to pin magic on them, but her husband had retaliated and she became paralysed and had remained in this condition. After the incident had been exposed and exorcism had been administered, she suddenly found she was able to move across the room and gradually her muscles became stronger. Neither spiritual nor natural healing could help her, because she needed to be loosed from the spirit of infirmity.*

I have tried to show the similarity between the instances in the Gospels where Jesus used exorcism and the cases where I have used exorcism in recent years. I was myself surprised to find how relevant the stories of the Gospels are to our modern life. We find today those who are possessed, oppressed and afflicted in the same way that Jesus did.

Exorcism and psychology

No doubt, many people will immediately put forward the argument that whereas Jesus used exorcism, we would use psychology today. Now this argument is totally false because it does not take into account the fact that many of the conditions mentioned are not cured by psychiatry and it is expert psychiatrists who are the first to admit it. Numerous doctors have sent me patients of recent years, including the late Dr. Moodie who sent me a patient direct from his consulting rooms in Harley Street. Dr. Frank Lake recently asked me to take part in a dialogue with him on the demonic and the psychological to a branch of the Institute of Religion and Medicine. It was interesting to discover that the doctors were far more open minded on the subject than the clergy and ministers. Dr. Lake explained that he considered that there was a driving force of destruction and seduction—a

* Luke 13: 11–15.

demonic force which affected people apart from psychological symptoms. He quoted a case where he had brought a patient of his to me for exorcism and could feel the force go out of him through the exorcism. He was then able to treat the patient more easily afterwards.

Diagnosis must decide

The fact is that in medieval times the tendency was to treat all kinds of conditions as diabolical, whilst a few years ago nearly everything abnormal was treated as psychological. What many doctors, clergy and social workers are coming to realise today is that what is really needed is a careful diagnosis of each condition to try and discover what treatment would answer the need. As I have already explained, I have had a number of requests from doctors, both in hospitals and outside, to see patients for exorcism.

It is most important, as a doctor pointed out to me, for doctors to recognise that there are some cases of schizophrenia and epilepsy which are essentially spiritual and will not be cured medically. In the same way, it is important that priests should recognise that they should not attempt exorcism where schizophrenia or epilepsy are due to medical conditions of the brain. That is why co-operation between doctors and clergy is so important in this sphere.

Exorcist and psychiatrist agree

Naturally, it is difficult to diagnose and mistakes are made on both sides. For myself, as I have explained, I have been able to discern by vibrations whether a person needed exorcism. To give an example of this, a young girl was sent to me by a psychiatrist for exorcism and in the interview I perceived vibrations and exorcised her. Shortly afterwards, a young man who knew the girl turned up to see me, saying that the same doctor had sent him for exorcism. I thought this was strange, as the doctor himself let me know about the girl, but I interviewed the man just the same. As the interview progressed, I began to realise that the young man had no vibrations and showed signs of psychological unbalance. I did not exorcise him but blessed him simply instead. I subsequently rang the doctor and discovered that the psychiatrist had not sent him at all, because he considered him a medical schizophrenic. In both cases, the independent diagnosis of the psychiatrist and myself entirely tallied.

Exorcism and medicine

A professor of medicine sent me a TV actor whom he considered needed help from exorcism, in spite of the fact that he had been receiving psychiatric treatment. A consultant psychiatrist asked me to use exorcism for a patient in the hospital chapel, but when I consulted the hospital chaplain, he was not keen for the Anglican chapel to be used so we used the Roman Catholic chapel instead. Some cases are both diabolical and psychological, and exorcism can have psychological side effects, so it is important to have close co-operation in the case of hospital patients particularly. I have found of recent years, that the old prejudices against exorcism are tending to disappear and many doctors and clergy who at one time tended to be wary of such a thing are openly recognising its place in dealing with people of abnormal behaviour. Of course, there are still many doctors who tend to consider such a thing as medieval simply because they are ill informed about its use and effects. Often they are rightly worried by its use by unrecognised healers who make elaborate claims. A bishop told me of a case of a man who was exorcised for headaches when he had a tumour on the brain. I fully sympathise with doctors because it was not carefully diagnosed. There is a growing awareness of the need for exorcism among the medical profession. Quite apart from doctors who have consulted me about patients I have also had the privilege of administering exorcism personally to doctors including psychiatrists as well as a number of medical auxiliaries and nurses.

Exorcism and the law

Another difficulty arises over culpability in law cases where "possession" is concerned. A barrister pointed out to me that there should be a clear distinction made between what is uncontrolled—indisciplined—and what is uncontrollable due to possession or some external force. Clearly there is a type of violence which is purely uncontrolled but there is also another type which is uncontrollable.

Take, for instance, the case of a man who attacked his fiancé and was tried at the Old Bailey. I was asked to make a written statement to be read by the judge but not cross-examined because part of what the man told me was under the seal of confession. His actions were considered out of character and temporarily uncontrollable so he was placed on probation rather than sent to prison and I was put in touch with the probation officer.

Another instance was that of a man who had been convicted of arson at the Old Bailey and was brought to the Court of Appeal for retrial. The Court of Appeal decided to release him on the grounds that a priest-exorcist, the late Rev. Gilbert Shaw, should act as surety for six months. Again they considered that the actions of the man were temporarily uncontrollable.

Another case was that of a young boy tried in a juvenile court for setting fire to a school. I was called as an expert witness to show that the boy had been involved in poltergeist activity in his home where fires had been caused and furniture flung around. The barrister presented the evidence along the lines that the mind did not follow the action, again uncontrollable and not purely uncontrolled. The court decided to put the child in care of the Council instead of sending him to Borstal, which could have been the case without the evidence of poltergeist activity. Actually it was mentioned in court that the poltergeist activity ceased after exorcism of the boy.*

Like the medical profession, there is also a growing awareness

* The Daily Express, March 9th 1971

among members of the legal profession that there is a need for exorcism in cases of possession. I have also had the privilege to minister exorcism personally to lawyers, both barristers and solicitors. Actually one of the barristers told me how he had been found in his chambers unconscious just after a difficult criminal case. The doctors could find no medical cause but he was unable to function for six months. He came to me because a barrister friend had told him he was suffering from a 'Satanic oppression'. After exorcism, he returned to function in the High Court within a few weeks.

Exorcism and architecture

So far in this chapter I have considered people, but I think it may be valuable to turn briefly to places. An eminent architect told me that when old houses were photographed for historic purposes, ghosts were often seen unexpectedly in the photograph. A peer's son told me how when he had stayed in different historic houses he was aware of ghosts without being told about them. I will consider this in a later chapter more fully. Recently an architect asked me to exorcise a house in the country because he considered the hauntings made it difficult to find an occupier. A surveyor asked me to exorcise a large building in Central London because a black magic cult had held their practices there and they now wanted to use it for flats. Here again we find a growing awareness among architects and surveyors of sensitivity to evil and the need of exorcism. I have had the privilege of ministering exorcism personally to architects, surveyors, engineers and designers.

I give these examples to show quite clearly that exorcism is becoming recognised as a professional practice by professional men and can no longer be regarded as a rather odd thing for 'cranks'. Nor can it be considered as something easily acceptable to gullible people. Actually highly intelligent art and book critics as well as TV producers and actors have been exorcised as well.

Exorcism–private

It should be recognised at the same time that normally the ministry of exorcism should be private like confession or unction and not used at a public service or with a group of people collected for a special occasion which can only embarrass the person. Close friends or religious communities may be asked to pray but they do not have to be present.

Exorcism should be regarded not so much as a rite of the Church but as an expression of the Gospel. If it is seen in its true perspective it should be within an ecumenical and sacramental setting. It is not something in isolation from prayer and sacraments yet not confined to the rite of a particular Church for its adherents.

Exorcism—ecumenical

I have had the privilege to minister exorcisms to numerous Roman Catholics from various parts of the world. Many Roman Catholic priests have welcomed this ministry and some Roman Catholic priests have even asked me for it themselves as well as asking about it for their people as many have no knowledge or experience of it. In some cases I have sent Roman Catholics to recognised Roman Catholic exorcists; others have been sent to me by them. I have also ministered to Russian and Greek Orthodox. I ministered to the Russian who had been imprisoned for his faith and suffered from oppression through it. I also ministered to a Greek Orthodox doctor and to a member of the Armenian Church sent to me by a doctor. I have also ministered to members of the Ethiopian Church, to Scandinavian and German Lutherans, Presbyterians, Methodists, Baptists, Congregationalists, Pentecostals and Quakers. They have accepted exorcism through me as a Priest and a minister of the Gospel without qualm or quibble. I have had the privilege to minister to over thirty Anglican priests, including a Missionary Bishop and also a Presbyterian minister. Methodist ministers and Congregational ministers have assisted me in exorcising their people and numerous Anglicans have also done so when they have brought people to me. I only mention these facts to illustrate the new ecumenical approach which is needed today.

Exorcism by the spirit

We cannot prepare people for exorcism in the same way as for baptism or confirmation as is suggested in the Exorcism Report.* Exorcism is something which meets an immediate need. Often a request springs from a prayerful decision and I am convinced that we should accept people as Our Lord did in the Gospel. We may have to challenge them to recognise sin in order to liberate them. Their condition is usually brought about by sin, not necessarily their own but perhaps the sin of someone else who has caused evil to enter into their life, perhaps through an act of violence or an assault. Part of their liberation often means a formal or informal confession. Often the reason why an exorcism appears to be ineffective is because the person has not made an open and honest confession.

Exorcism not alone

I do not believe that exorcism is always the answer to people who request it from me. Sometimes I find they need unction or healing. Sometimes they need to learn to pray and meditate. One man told me I saw a devil in everyone but this is a travesty of the truth. I have been an ordinary parish priest who at one time had an Electoral Roll of 200 but only exorcised 2 out of 200, but ministered to them all in other ways.

Exorcism when it is used should never be seen in isolation as a form of magic but should be followed up by prayer and sacrament. Sometimes exorcism breaks through the blockage in prayer and opens up new ways of meditation or worship or perhaps a return to communion. Sometimes it releases faith

* Exorcism Report, p. 24. Edited by Don Robert Petitpierre.

and leads to baptism or confirmation. Sometimes it makes possible a decision for marriage or ordination. The devil is always trying to attack vocations. Fr. Gilbert Shaw used to say that the devil took a particular interest in trying to ruin priests. A priest of some standing recently said to me that after a few exorcisms, he felt an entirely new liberation—not purely *from* evil forces, but *for* the work and service of God.

CHAPTER 3

WITH AUTHORITY AND POWER HE COMMANDETH*—RENUNCIATION

Witch-force and Christ

When I was recording a tape with a B.B.C. interviewer, he suddenly asked me "What does it feel like to have a power which other people have not got"? I replied by saying "I have not got a power which other people cannot use, it's God's power and if I ever forgot it, I would lose it." Now this is fundamental to all spiritual work but particularly so in the realm of exorcism. Fr. Gilbert Shaw strongly emphasised to me the enormous importance of differentiating between the spiritual and the psychic. In a recent TV programme "The Power of the Witch",** in which I participated in exorcising a man who had been bewitched, the psychic power used by the witch—the witch-force or psychic force—was very well illustrated. However, it should be stated firmly that this force is not on the same wavelength as power used by Christ. 'Witchcraft' which is sometimes considered to be a 'fertility cult' derives its power from natural forces like the moon (white), or in some of its more sinister forms through 'devil-worship' (black).

* Luke 4: 36.
** December 15th, 1971.

Witch-force still here

The Daily Mirror reckons that there are 40,000 witches in Britain today—30,000 white and 10,000 black.* Many young people are drawn into witchcraft without fully realising the consequences of their action. Some have sought it to gain power over others through hidden means. The evidence seems to suggest that witchcraft and black magic are present day facts and not past fancies.**

However, Sir Alexander Haddow (in a letter to the Times entitled Exorcism in the Church), states "I am moderately acquainted with the ancient history of exorcism . . . we must acknowledge the likely existence of phenomena outside our ken, but this does not compel us to accept black magic or witchcraft.†"

In a similar way Dr. Carr, a psychiatrist from West Park Hospital, when he commented on my TV film on Exorcism the following night, said that witchcraft was 300 years out of date.††

What is surprising is that both Sir Alexander Haddow and Dr. Carr appear to disregard the practice of modern witchcraft and seem to have no idea of what is happening in our midst. Their views clearly reflect the attitude of many people who are unaware of the living reality of witchcraft and black magic and the impact of the forces surrounding them.

When I appeared on "Nationwide" in relation to a report concerning exorcism in Mental Hospitals, Michael Barrett asked me whether I considered it dangerous to use exorcism for mental patients. I replied by pointing out that in some cases it would be dangerous if it were *not* used.‡ I was once asked by a Chaplain to a Mental Hospital to see a girl who had been taken in because she had made quite a few suicide attempts. It transpired that she had been a victim of witchcraft, and after the exorcism with a renunciation of the past, the suicide thoughts were dispelled. Clearly it would have been dangerous if she had not been exorcised.

* Daily Mirror, February 28th, 1972.
**See MODERN WITCHCRAFT, Smyth.
† The Times, July 22nd, 1972.
†† June 16th, 1971.
‡ June 9th, 1971.

Spirituality not psychiatry

In the previous chapter, I have shown cases in which I have had the co-operation of psychiatrists—cases which needed careful diagnosis because of the pressures on the mind and behaviour of the person—but it must now be clearly stated that there are a large number of cases requiring exorcism which have no bearing on psychiatry at all. It is a very limited view held in the Exorcism report which suggests that cases of 'possession' should not be undertaken without psychiatric advice. Such a view tends to decry the 'discernment of spirits'.* The recent growth of humanism in this country has tended in the view of one critic to make 'psychiatry the humanist's religion'. I have recently had the privilege of ministering exorcism to Indians, West Indians, and Africans and it never occurs to them to even mention psychiatry because they are perceptively aware that their condition is one of the spirit and not essentially of the mind at all. Witch-forces or black magic or departed spirits are a matter of spirituality, not psychiatry. The wise psychiatrist sends people suffering from such influences to a priest, but a psychiatrist who attempts to treat them makes confusion worse confounded. Britain seems to be so psychologically conditioned that many people fail to see its limitations. The late Dr. R. I. Milne, Coroner for North London, once pointed out that many of the cases of suicide which came to his court had been treated quite ineffectually by psychiatrists. He stated that 'renewal of faith' was in his view the only answer to suicide and that many of these people might have been helped more by a priest or minister.

Psychic perceptiveness with Afro-Asians

No doubt, many may say that Indians, West Indians or Africans are conditioned by primitive animist (belief in spirits) ideas. With the growth of education in these lands, this argument is no longer valid. In fact, those to whom I have ministered have been largely highly intelligent professional men or students, many of

* Exorcism Report, p. 23.

whom have a far greater critical faculty than some of the simpler English I have seen. The fact is that Indians, West Indians and Africans have a far more penetrating psychic perceptiveness than many Europeans. I have often been approached by Africans or West Indians in the Universal Prayer Group or Indians individually who have themselves discerned the personality of the spirit who is attached to them or the particular person who put a force on them. Whereas, many English suffering from a similar condition are often quite unable to discern who the attached spirit is or from whom the force emanated. It is this lack of psychic perceptiveness which makes exorcism of the English far more difficult. It also tends to deny such forces because of psychological conditioning.

In the previous chapter, we have considered cases of people who were largely unconscious of the evil forces which gripped them. In this chapter, I am endeavouring to show cases of people who have willfully and willingly linked themselves to covens or cults in order to develop powers or derive benefit from the witch-force or psychic power. I have also given examples of victims of witchcraft or black magic who have suffered through involvement with those who practise it. It is not generally recognised that those who are initiated into witchcraft are given a witch name and some claim that they have been married to the devil. I have also tried to illustrate witchcraft in Britain in the wider context of witchcraft from various parts of the world.

Solemn exorcisms by priests

In the TV programme I have just mentioned, a Church Army Captain explained how he did splendid work in exorcising young initiates and victims of witchcraft. At the same time, it should be recognised that an experienced witch would only recognise a priest of the Church equivalent to her own high priest or high priestess. Such authority would not be accorded to a layman. In any case the sacraments as well as exorcism would be needed. There is a special 'priestcraft' (if you like), to deal with witches which should be explained. The question is asked "What is thy name?" and when the witch's name is given, the priest asks "Who am I?" and the witch answers "God's priest." Then follows the solemn renunciation "Dost thou renounce the devil and all his works?" Now Fr. Gilbert Shaw was most insistent and I entirely concur with him that a solemn exorcism of this nature should only be undertaken by a priest speaking in the name of Christ and with the authority of his Church. It is not purely an individual gift or power except in so far as a particular priest may be especially authorised for it, but it is the authority of Christ given to his Apostles and not to all and sundry however holy or gifted they may be. The Church has always differentiated between solemn or simple exorcism and whereas solemn exorcism is only undertaken by the priest, simple exorcism is sometimes undertaken by laymen. For instance, Fr. Poulain, S. J., states "Solemn exorcisms are performed in Church. Priests alone can undertake them. Private exorcisms are always permitted even to the laity."* Fr. Tanquerey also states "The solemn exorcism has been restricted to priests. However, lay persons may recite exorcism prayers."**

Agents and victims

In the same way, in dealing with witchcraft, there should be a clear differentiation between agents and victims. In the case of an agent there should be a firm resolve to make a final renunciation before exorcism takes place. It is not always recognised that an initiate in some forms of witchcraft is expected to renounce his or her baptismal vow, so it is important for a witch in returning to or entering the Church to renew or make the baptismal vows, the first of which is to 'renounce the devil and all his works.'

It is interesting to see how baptism and exorcism have been connected through the ages and the only fully recognised form of exorcism is that contained in the Baptism Service in the 1549

* Graces of Interior Prayer, Poulain, p. 431.
** The Spiritual Life, Tanquerey, p. 724.

Book of Common Prayer. The Decision, in the New Baptism Service 1967 is particularly relevant as it contains three vows:

1) I turn to Christ.
2) I repent of my sins.
3) I renounce evil.

On one occasion, a priest brought me a man who had practised devil worship and witchcraft in Latin America. He claimed during the interview that he did not believe in God, but whilst we were doing the exorcism he suddenly shouted spontaneously "I believe in God." So we took him immediately to the font and baptised him, where he formally renounced the devil and all his works and repeated the short baptismal creed. It reminded us of Philip and the Ethiopian eunuch.*

Where no actual devil worship is involved the renunciation of evil can be used instead. In some cases of witchcraft, it is a departed witch who has 'bewitched' the woman concerned and the departed witch has to renounce her witchcraft before the living person can be finally cleared. In cases of black witchcraft, the words, 'renounce the devil', should be used.

Cases of witchcraft in England

One of the strangest cases of witchcraft was that of an apparently devout communicant member of a Church who from time to time became unusually virulent towards her parish priest without any reasonable cause. The parish priest became suspicious when the psychiatrist whom she was attending and also a consultant psychiatrist whom she had seen both suddenly died within a matter of weeks. At the same time the priest's wife developed signs of cancer. At the priest's invitation, I challenged the woman and discovered after exorcisms that she had a lifelong friend who was a 'Queen Witch' controlling a number of covens and lodges. This Queen Witch had clearly bewitched the woman who was acting as an agent of destruction. First I was able to

* Acts 8: 37, 38.

exorcise and anoint the priest's wife, who was cleared of cancer. However, the Queen Witch after death continued to possess and use this woman as an agent to cause trouble. Then, through automatic writing given to the woman, the Queen Witch asked for spiritual help from me. Finally I challenged her departed spirit; she renounced her witchcraft at the altar and left the woman in peace.

Another instance is that of an old woman whom a parish priest asked me to see as he suspected witchcraft. On being challenged, she admitted that she had been branded and initiated as a witch when she was a young girl. She was possessed by a departed witch spirit (a gypsy), who spoke through her in a deep voice apparently coming from her stomach. She first accused the parish priest of an immoral act some years before, of which she had no natural knowledge, and accused me of coming to destroy her. Then in the exorcism, the spirit left her and her face visibly changed. We took her to the font and she renounced the devil and was baptised.

Two high priestesses

A High Priestess of a witch coven who claimed to have been married to the devil came to me. She had actually been a communicant before entering the coven. She used confession as evidence of repentance and received absolution before making her renunciation. When it came to the actual exorcism, she physically threw my hands away from her head, but I took them and put them in the form of a cross and she collapsed temporarily unconscious. When she was brought round with holy water, she got up and turned as if to leave the church, but took the wrong turning and found herself kneeling in front of the statue of Our Lady weeping as she had not wept for years. The witch-force had dissolved. She told me afterwards that the voice of a departed witch told her during the exorcism "Don't let him put his hands on your head" and that is why she resisted. This was very interesting evidence that the power of exorcism comes through the hands and that the departed witch caused the resistance. She lost all resistance when the departed witch was cleared from her.

In the case of another High Priestess connected with white witchcraft there was no attempt to use any evil force against me. She had been the victim of a curse by another witch who wanted to marry her. The reason was that she had refused him and become engaged to another man who was outside witchcraft. I lifted the curse through exorcism and after she had renounced witchcraft, I had the privilege of solemnising her marriage with a nuptial mass, as she had previously been a communicant.

I know from experience of exorcising high priests and high priestesses of witch covens that the witch-force has a rather rare intensity not found in ordinary exorcisms. I acknowledge the 'power of the witch' as a real phenomenon in our midst which we disregard at our peril. Alex Saunders commonly called "King of the Witches" claims to have initiated 4,000 witches in this country today. He also claims to have renounced black witchcraft. I am fully prepared to recognise that many of those who practise witchcraft have no evil intent in themselves. However, we have to reckon with the fact that anyone who uses powers over others is in danger of being used by the devil even if they do not themselves worship him. The witches who have come to me freely desired the help of the Church because they became aware of such dangers from others or within themselves.

On one occasion a witch who had left a coven came to me in a desperate state because other members of the coven, which claimed to be white, had used witch forces to pull her back. We bound the members of the coven and loosed her from them.

Worldwide interest

Apart from B.B.C. Television programmes I have mentioned, I have also done two television films for other parts of the world and each film included an exorcism of a victim of witchcraft and the interviews hinged round questions of witchcracft. One of these programmes was under the auspices of the Italian State Television, with interpreters, and the other was undertaken by C.B.S. Television from U.S.A.

The Italian TV film included items by others from India and the Middle East as well as other parts of Europe. Since I did this film, I have had two Italians come to see me for exorcism. One of them said that witchcraft had affected his walking and he found it difficult to travel but claimed after the exorcisms that he could control his muscles. The other one claimed that relatives had used witchcraft on him in Italy and he had retaliated by using a witch against them. I told him that he must renounce the use of witchcraft and he told the witch to cease. His wife and family had to be exorcised as well as himself before the witch-force was cleared.

I have also had a man fly especially from Belgium and a woman from North Germany both requesting exorcism from me because of witchcraft. Both said they felt the witch-force lift from them through exorcism. A Frenchman who had witchcraft put on him whilst working in Paris saw me for exorcism only a few hours before flying to Paris because he was so desperate. These examples, and I could give many others, reflect the prevalent practice of witchcraft in different parts of Europe.

The C.B.S. TV film which included an item from the Universal Prayer Group of West Indians and Africans to whom I minister was shown from coast to coast in the U.S.A. and syndicated to Australia and New Zealand.* I have received numerous letters from various parts of the U.S.A., in States as far apart as California, Florida and Pennsylvania, again revealing the practice of witchcraft. Two different American women requested exorcism for witchcraft, each on their way through London to Europe. One came straight from Heathrow Airport and returned there a few hours later to continue her flight. I also had a woman from Australia and one from New Zealand visit me for exorcism whilst they were in London because they were affected by witch-forces.

* May 6th, 1972.

I also did a hot-line broadcast to Melbourne referring to a case of witchcraft.

Wolf-cult

When I did a similar hot-line broadcast to Toronto on a programme "As it Happens" I referred to the case of a young man who was initiated into a 'wolf-cult'—as part of the Red Indian rites in Canada*. The purpose of the cult was to acquire and use the characteristics of the wolf. He had also been a high priest in a coven in this country. After he had renounced the cult I exorcised him and the force left him. He was subsequently confirmed in the Church.

African voodoo

I have also broadcast on 'Africa' radio in conjunction with our African group. This group is well acquanted with African witchcraft, one example of which is 'voodoo'. One night at **3 a.m.** I had a telephone call from a West African member of our African group saying that he was being killed by voodoo. I could hear his breathing getting weaker and quickly used an exorcism over the telephone which gave him immediate relief and I was then able to release him through exorcism the following day. He asserted that another member of the Group was using this which I must admit I found difficult to believe, but the said member actually arrived on my doorstep within 24 hours. I challenged him and he admitted he had been using witchcraft. I asked him when he had used it and he said "3 a.m." He finally renounced it by bringing his books on witchcraft and 'black arts' and they were burnt in the churchyard.

The distinction made between witchcraft and black magic is largely a matter of religious ritual. Witchcraft is bound up with religious ritual whilst black magic is a secular method of using the same force.

* TV "24 Hours," June 20th, 1969.

West Africa

The power of binding and loosing evil is given to the Church: "Whatsoever thou shalt bind on earth, shall be bound in heaven, and whatsoever thou shalt loose on earth, shall be loosed in heaven."* A West African barrister told me that she had seen in her dreams certain relatives using witchcraft against her from West Africa, attempting to maim her womb and make her barren. I placed their names on the altar and bound the forces coming through them by the power of the 'living God, the true God, the holy God, in the name of the Father and the Son and the Holy Ghost' and then loosed her by the 'sword of the Holy Spirit' in exorcism, by cutting the psychic links with her relatives. She told me later that the force which was being used against her had ceased completely. She had recovered from the pains she had been suffering. They were, so to speak, bound over in the court of heaven.

West Indian obeah

A young West Indian told me that his father had tried to put a 'spell' on him ("obeah" as it is called in the West Indies). Like voodoo or witchcraft in Africa this type of spell appears to be quite common in the West Indies. Apparently out of jealousy his father had tried to stop him progressing as a student by this spell. I bound his father at the altar in the same way and the young man had a vision of his father 'bound by cords' and felt a release through exorcism from the force which had been inhibiting his studies. The Africans and West Indians have a very clear perception into these psychic forces which some sophisticated English find difficult to accept. I have used the exorcism of binding and loosing for hundreds of them in this country. I have also bound and loosed the evil forces from English people with similar effect. I bound the witch-force from a Cornish woman on a London lawyer and he felt a sudden release. Some priests talk about

* St. Matthew 16: 19.

'binding Satan' but there is no reference to this in the Bible except of an angel binding Satan.* There is no suggestion that priests or ministers should do it.

Power of the Church

Jesus gave to St. Peter the 'keys of the Kingdom'—the power of binding and loosing of evil as it emanates from those on earth,—"whatsoever thou shalt bind on earth shall be bound in heaven."** Therefore, the priest acting in the name of the Church, binds the evil forces of witchcraft, sorcery or black magic, by restraining the person from using them. He binds the force by putting the name of the person using it on the altar or mentioning his name at the altar, but he does *not* bind Satan himself. This 'binding' may well bring a person to penitence—it may shake him into submission to God, but it does no physical harm. It is the 'bands of love' which makes them aware of evil and sin.

Witchcraft in Africa has been practised for centuries and it is of a far more sinister kind than is usually practised in this country. Many African and West Indian students in this country find that relatives from 'back home', as they call it, try to interfere with their studies through jealousy—perhaps half sisters or half brothers who have not had the same opportunities themselves. I thought it seemed exaggerated when special prayers were made for exminations. I have subsequently discovered that such prayers are essential. They are a protection against the witch forces transmitted telepathically by jealous relatives or acquaintances from beyond the seas.

Witch's curse

As we have already mentioned the 'witch's curse', it might be valuable to give an example of it from Africa. An English

* Rev. 20: 2.
** Matt. 16: 19.

missionary and his wife went out to Africa where a witch put a curse on their marriage. They ignored it for some years and later they returned on furlough to this country. The wife suddenly refused to go back with her husband and they parted. The wife came to see me in a grief-stricken state. I bound the evil forces and abrogated the curse. After this exorcism, she received a letter from her husband offering reconciliation and within a week or so she had flown back to Africa to rejoin her husband.

Indian kali

We find another sinister form of witchcraft emanating from India. An Indian Christian came to see me because he said he had been the victim of witchcraft which his grandfather and father had practised. They were Hindus but he had broken away from the tradition to become a Christian. This witchcraft, 'Kali' as he called it, was used to destroy his marriage and business. Exorcism helped to clear him from it.

However, when we turn to India we naturally turn from witchcraft to black magic. One priest claimed that three quarters of the magic of the world is found in the Himalayas. One instance of black magic is that of an Indian prince who 'captivated' an exiled European princess. This sounds like a fairy tale if it were not so horribly true. The exiled princess was forlorn having left her country and husband. At that point through correspondence and later through a powerful form of magic, the Indian prince literally captivated her soul until she could not think freely. By binding the forces of magic, she suddenly found a new freedom and independence. Another instance was that of a young man who had been in an Indian 'ashram' under a guru and after disagreement with the guru left it. The guru lured the young man into an illicit affair with his daughter in England who seduced him. Then the guru by a powerful form of magic from India exerted a control over the young man's mind. By binding the forces, the young man found a new freedom of mind.

Egyptian magic

Another form of black magic emanates from Egypt. I had a case of a woman who was captivated by an Egyptian doctor who had first treated her and then appeared to place magic on her. She became obsessed by Egyptian things and was drawn to visit museums where she could find them. I bound the forces coming through this doctor and she was liberated from this strange mysterious force.

Japanese magic

Another case of black magic emanated from Japan. An English girl became engaged to a Japanese man of Moslem background who had been brought up in a Christian school. The family of the Japanese tried to use black magic to break up their engagement. After the girl was exorcised and later confirmed, she was married to the Japanese man in my church and the spell was broken.

Pakistani magic

Another case emanating from the East is that of a Pakistani doctor. An English doctor working in a hospital approached me for exorcism because he felt an evil force causing him to lose concentration and he feared he might cause harm to a patient. It was then discovered that a Pakistani doctor had been jealous of him and had used black magic against him. When he was exorcised, his concentration and equilibrium were restored.

Black magic in England

Black magic is, of course, frequently used in this country. Take the example of a business man whose secretary left him after she had had an affair. Because of the hold he had on her, he used black magic and destroyed her concentration, making it impossible for her to work. When we had bound the forces, she used confession and was later confirmed after which the evil forces subsided completely. Another girl was seduced by a girl who was Lesbian. The Lesbian then used black magic through the hold she had on her and drove her into a complete nervous breakdown. After the whole thing was exposed through confession and exorcism, the evil forces dissolved and she regained her confidence.

Spiritualism

People often wonder how the forces of black magic work. They do not realise that it is done through a powerful form of telepathy. The police asked me to investigate two cases of black magic. One was that of a young man who claimed another man was using it against him. The other was that of a girl who had asked for police protection. There was evidence in the case of the young man, but in the girl's case it was fear rather than the actual force. Quite apart from witchcraft and black magic, many people are born with strong psychic powers which can be used telepathically. I know two cases of women who had great gifts of telepathy and healing but each was distorted in their ministry by using healing on someone who was morally corrupted. The sad thing was that evil seemed to grip their souls because they were using psychic gifts without surrendering them to God. Their whole lives were disrupted through it. This shows how important it is that a distinction between psychic and spiritual healing should be firmly grasped. If a person dedicates his gifts to God then he will sublimate them and the person will become a channel of God's power. If he attempts to use his own powers, then he opens the way to evil forces through pride and lack of dependence on God. How often have people come to me after they have been to spiritualistic healers because they are not made whole. The fact is that sometimes the spiritualist healer proudly makes large claims to heal but in fact some of the people are physically healed but psychically disturbed and that is why they asked for exorcism.

Beware spiritualism

People are often attracted to spiritualism through the death of a dear one and persuaded to attend a séance or meeting. They begin by contacting the departed but it often happens that before long an evil spirit has made contact with them and distorted or disturbed their whole life. As I have said earlier I am not prejudiced against careful psychic research. What I am describing is the condition of people who through sensitive imagination have been caught by departed or discarnate spirits and it would have been better for them if they had never had anything to do with spiritualism at all. I have had hundreds of requests for help from people who have contacted departed spirits, but not all these need exorcism. In some cases it is a requiem said for the soul. In other cases it is a prayer of commendation of the soul, or a direct charging of the spirit.

One strange case was that of a man medium who at one time was functioning at the Spiritualist Association. The mediums who had co-operated with him could not help him and he asked me to get rid of a spirit by exorcism. This illustrated very clearly that mediums are not always able to drive away spirits in spite of the claims that are made. The medium may discover a spirit and persuade it to leave, but the priest can command it and he may even have to absolve the departed spirit first, or charge it and bind it. This cannot be done by a medium.

Discernment of spirits

I think it is important to point out that it is necessary for the priest to have the discernment of spirits and to be guided by the Holy Spirit. This is what Francoise Strachan describes as an intuitive exorcist.* If a priest charges the departed spirit, he demands its name and the reason why it is present. The medium often gets a name which is quite erroneous and often makes confusion worse confounded. In two cases where a young man had

* Casting out the Devils, Francoise Strachan, p. 37.

consulted a medium, the departed spirit remained because the name the medium gave had no relation to the person. I discovered from each man that it was the departed spirit of an uncle, a wicked uncle—who in one case had been a drunkard and in the other case a homosexual. In one case the medium had got the Christian name but called him some other surname which made nonsense to the man and got nowhere. I challenged the actual uncle by name, who was a departed spirit in each case. On one occasion the spirit acknowledged his faults and was absolved. Then I drew away the departed spirit and drove out the demon, or *δαιμων*. Another priest had tried to drive out the demon without charging the spirit but this was ineffectual.

Absolutions of the dead

A man once approached me because he said his wife was possessed by the spirit of a neighbour who had shot himself. Before I exorcised his wife, I charged the spirit, absolved him and commanded him to depart and she felt an immediate release. The traditional service of Absolutions for the Dead can be seen in a new setting—"Absolve O Lord their souls from every bond of sin," this soul was earthbound because he had tried to murder his wife and then shot himself. Fr. Durrance, an exorcist from Florida, actually baptises people for the dead on the grounds that the spirits which possess them are not baptised. Personally, I am convinced that St. Paul attacks this practice and it is an erroneous tradition.* In contrast, Absolutions of the Dead is traditional throughout the ages of the Church and often combined with Requiem; both are badly needed to deal with modern situations regarding departed spirits. People need to have a deeper spiritual understanding than purely the formal ritual.

Possession by departed

One of the difficulties of dealing with departed spirits is the fact that the departed spirit may be possessed by a demon. Con-

* 1 Cor. 15: 29.

sequently evil comes through the departed spirit, who is not as benign as is supposed. Sometimes there is an overshadowing of a near relative like a father or mother. One case was that of a man who had been sadistically treated by his father. After his father's death, the man became violent in physically assaulting people, was charged and imprisoned. After he came out, psychiatry could do nothing for him and he suddenly became aware that he might be possessed by the demonic forces emanating from his father's spirit. Exorcism gave him a quite remarkable release.

One remarkable case was that of an Indian who had become a Christian from a Hindu background. He was haunted by his departed father who was a Hindu priest and tried to draw him back to the old Hindu religion. I charged the spirit and by challenging him in the name of Christ brought him into the holy light. The Indian found peace.

Young people today often have a hang-up about their parents and this seems to continue even after a parent has died. Billy Graham says that a hippie has been defined as "someone who loves everyone except his parents."* A young man only found peace when he was reconciled to his departed father at the altar and his father's soul was set at peace.

A priest told me how he had been overshadowed by his grandfather who had been a drunkard. This blood-link seemed to pull him in the same direction. By setting his grandfather at rest by drawing his spirit away and then driving out the demon, (or *δαιμων* he found a new freedom, he was no longer tied to Bacchus, (the god of wine).

A young woman seemed dominated by suicidal thoughts for no apparent reason. It was discovered that her grandfather had committed suicide and his spirit seemed to overshadow her. When his spirit was drawn away, she lost these desperate states and found a new lease of life.

* THE JESUS GENERATION, Graham, p. 52.

Overshadowing

An 'overshadowing' is when a departed spirit is attached to the person, or the aura of the person if you like. The psychic link has to be cut and the person must themselves give up the affinity with the departed spirit if they really intend to make a new start. Some people find this particularly difficult and often exorcism has to be repeated until the discarnate spirit finally departs.

Ouija boards—like smoking

Sometimes, a discarnate or departed spirit is called up or brought up through the use of a ouija-board. Now, I often regard the use of the ouija boards or the glass game as it used to be called in the same way as some people regard smoking. Many people may not be affected by smoking at all, but the odd one develops lung cancer. Many may use ouija boards and nothing may occur but the odd one catches a spirit. That is why it is important to be warned about ouija boards as it is about smoking.

I know of one young man whose whole life was nearly ruined through using a ouija board. The spirit of a girl latched on to him and caused him to be violent to a girl friend. The girl friend was taken to hospital with a broken arm and the young man was not permitted to see her. I went to the hospital with him and explained the matter to the psychiatrist who them relented.

Another example was that of a teenage girl who played the glass game with one of her schoolmates. A spirit of a teacher who had died appeared and told her she would be killed in an air crash. The sad thing was that she had to go abroad by air to her parents. She was naturally terrified, but after I had exorcised her, she lost the fear, went on the plane and was perfectly safe.

Another case was one of a young girl of Jewish background who had been to a séance at the age of twelve. She had been affected by nightmares of departed spirits for two years afterwards but was cleared through exorcism.

Ghosts

It seems appropriate at this point to turn to 'ghosts'. I draw a distinction here between departed spirits who attach themselves to people and ghosts who appear independently in houses or places to a number of people without in any way attaching themselves to a person. Now there are many ghosts who are purely 'place memories' in old buildings who do no harm to the inhabitants. When I spoke to the Ghost Club which meets in the Constitutional Club, I was criticised for driving away what they called friendly ghosts. I think this was a misunderstanding; I am not really concerned with so-called friendly ghosts, only those who interfere with and intrude on people.

I was called to a house in Hampstead where three au pair girls had left because each said they had seen a ghost in the room where they were sleeping. I went there at midnight and saw clearly a young girl in Victorian dress. I asked her why she was there and she explained that she was a Lesbian and had attacked the girls because it used to be her room. I absolved and exorcised the ghost. Later the lady of the house asked the psychic research society to investigate the house because she wished to sell it. They could find no ghost; she had gone.

I was asked to go to a flat in Kensington where a ghost had been seen by three different people who presented their independent written evidence. I felt the presence of the ghost in one of the rooms which could have been where a former resident had died and I set her soul at rest. The lady who owned the flat wrote a short while afterwards and said that the alien personality had entirely disappeared.

People often claim that they do not believe in ghosts, but belief in this context seems to be inappropriate. A doctor I know takes sensitivity tests and so it can be said, as I have previously mentioned, that acknowledging ghosts could well be a matter of sensitivity rather than belief. Two people of differing sensitivity might enter a room; one would be conscious of the ghost, the other would not. What a person cannot perceive, he might easily tend to decry.

At the same time, we cannot lose sight of the fact that people do have hallucinations, perhaps due to drugs or drink, and for a ghost to be seriously considered it should be seen or experienced by more than one person.

Drugs

Drugs is another point through which evil enters. Francoise Strachan says: "Large quantities of L.S.D. actually shatter the aura, so that there is no protection and possession is almost simultaneous . . . drugs tend to open psychic centres."* I have had two cases of young men affected by L.S.D. They both seemed to go through a sort of identity crisis in which neither of them seemed to know what their true nature was. Each had self destructive tendencies apparently through contact with discarnate spirits. One of them asked for baptism and said he felt a quite new experience of warmth come through his Confirmation, which gave a new spiritual understanding. The other seemed tormented by negative impulses and needed a large number of exorcisms over a long period before he could find any spiritual strength.

Another young man took heroin and nearly died through it. He was exorcised, later confirmed and renewed his marriage vows because his marriage was in jeopardy. I met him some years later and he claimed that he had been free for eight years from heroin. From the look of his eyes and his general bearing it was clearly true. He even said the exorcism had brought back his memory.

One young man who came to me had been connected with a group of drug addicts. The others of his group had been arrested when he was fortunately away. He had a mask of the god Pan, who might well be called the god of drugs, in his room. In desperation he asked to be baptised as well as exorcised. Now, with the mask destroyed, the sign of the Cross protects him against evil.

* Casting out Devils, Strachan, p. 91.

Voices

One of the most difficult phenomena to deal with is 'voices'. Clearly there are those who have "voices" in the head which is a medical condition and treated by drugs. There are also those who have 'voices in the aura', a condition which is brought about by spirits talking to the person. An enlightened psychiatrist sent a woman to me for exorcism because he said she had voices in the aura and could not be treated by medical means. In her case, the voices ceased after the exorcism. Clearly, this condition needs very careful diagnosis. I am convinced that 'voices in the aura' spring from contact with departed spirits. Elderly people often seem to cultivate this condition and once they have contracted the habit of listening to voices it is very difficult to break. Sometimes it is the voice of a dear one,—husband or brother or sister,— and they seem to feel guilty about it, but they are only half-hearted in the desire to eradicate it. How often have I exorcised voices and within a matter of days or even hours the person says that the voices have returned or that they never really left them. The fact is that many old people would be lonely without their voices. In their better moments, they say that they would like them removed, but unconsciously they really want them. Sometimes people say there are a number of voices and they do not know who they are. However, on deeper investigation, it is often found that there is one predominant voice,—one spirit who provides the link which brings others in. Often the voice is that of an old boy friend or girl friend who is departed. It is a play on a memory but it is not purely imagination, for it is the actual departed spirit in contact with the person. The person must be made to recognise that once the exorcism has taken place, it is within the person's power to stop listening to the voices. 'God helps those who help themselves, as I am constantly telling people in relation to exorcism. People often ask me what success I have with different cases. Personally, I do not like to use the word success, because it is God's power, not mine. It would be better to use the word effective and if the person is open to God, then remarkable results, even miracles, occur.

Takes time

For instance, one middle-aged man who had been released from a demonic force which had gripped him through the discarnate spirit of a dead relative wrote:

> "*I am still wondering whether it can really have happened but as the days go by, I am becoming convinced that, to use a much abused word, a miracle in the sphere of the spirit and mind, a dimension with which I have become sadly out of touch, has taken place. The whole atmosphere at home has changed and for the first time for literally years, I have known release from what has seemed an almost constant unhappy sense of being tormented.*"

A young African student who had failed his examinations because he was inhibited by a demonic fear for which he had asked for exorcism wrote:

> "*Since my last visit to you early this week, I have noticed my self-confidence gradually coming back and fear disappearing from my day to day activity.*"

It is sometimes not recognised that it takes time for evil forces to fade and this man expressed this and emphasised the fact that he noticed it when he was not necessarily looking for it. People should not look for results, but go about their life without thinking about what may have happened. It is often then that they become surprised at themselves and what has happened, sometimes not at all what they had expected, but far more wonderful things than they could have expected. A young mother who had been disturbed about her marriage wrote after exorcism:

> "*Already I feel completely at peace with myself and that terrible fear and desperation have gone and I know in myself they will not return. Now I have a new strength.*"

An American man who came especially to London for exorcism wrote to me some months after his return to U.S.A.:

> "*As you said whilst I was in London, it would take three or four months for things to settle after the exorcisms. I feel better and I am getting more insight every day. It was a great revelation to me to find out that I was suffering from a disease of the spirit.*"

Spiritual sponges

You can see clearly from these instances that exorcism brings positive results—new spiritual strength, new insights, renewed self-confidence and even opens a new spiritual dimension. In contrast, however, there is always the 'spiritual sponge'—or hypochondriac in the spiritual sphere,—the person who goes round from spiritual healer to spiritual healer or exorcist to exorcist talking about his condition without ever facing the weakness in himself which is the real cause of his trouble and consequently finding no release. It is always easy to blame the devil for causing it or the exorcist for failing to remove it rather than facing the stark reality of sin. "Be not deceived, God is not mocked."* One man came to see me after he had been using witchcraft. I cleared him and warned him to renounce it but he came back and said he had done it again. A woman asked me to clear a spirit after using a ouija board, then used it again. Due to their failure in renunciation, their conditions returned.

True or false

At the same time, St. Joan of Arc had her 'voices' and these were true revelations. Let us remember that the true spiritual guides are the angels and the saints rather than Red Indian chiefs or Chinese doctors. I myself have heard the voice of St. Thérèse at her shrine at Lisieux when I went on a pilgrimage. Spirit communication, whether through voices, séances or circles, often

* Gal. 6: 7.

deceives or disturbs rather than helps a person. A spiritual revelation often needs interpretation by the spiritual director, but if it is truly from God it will bring calmness and confidence in place of perturbation and often leads to a true vocation.

Scientology and Hypnosis

There is a widespread interest today in meditation, hypnotism and schemes of training like scientology, but many do not realise the dangers of using the psychic without the spiritual discipline of the Church and the sacraments.

There was a civil servant who was 'processed' in scientology and later became involved in the organisation itself. He suddenly became aware of being controlled and left it. He asked to see me for exorcism, as he said he needed liberation, but he first made a renunciation.

A young man once appeared on my doorstep off the train from the north of England saying he had been hypnotised and was 'controlled' by a man who lived near him. I told him he would have to renounce all contact with this man and be exorcised as he originally intended. The hypnotic power was so strong that he said he could not pursue this and started to leave my house. I told him quite categorically that if he returned without exorcism I would not see him again. He went but returned twenty minutes later. He then pleaded with me to exorcise him at once and he was cleared. I quite recognise that there are forms of hypnotism in medical hands which are most valuable in bringing out hidden secrets and no doubt a sort of processing which could develop the personality, but people do not realise the dangers of such methods in unscrupulous hands.

Dangers of meditation

Many forms of meditation have become popular today which have no connection with the Church. It is a very good thing that there is this seeking for spirituality but there are also dangers in it. For instance, 'transcendental meditation' taught by Maharishi Mahesh Yogi has aroused widespread interest among Christians and non-Christians alike. There was an actor who went out to the Himalayas and lectured on this meditation. Unfortunately through opening his 'psyche' an evil force entered his consciousness, caused him to lose concentration and he became disturbed. Through exorcism, he was cleared and went into retreat where he found new strength. An Indian lecturer (who had become a Christian), told me he thought it was so strange for English students to use Hindu meditations because he had found from a Hindu background that it was far better to meditate on 'the Christ'. He went on to say that such students did not know what they were missing in Christianity. Christ is being revealed today as the 'Cosmic Christ' who appeals to the world,—the Saviour of the world* and the light of the world.**

The Cosmic Christ

I have been amazed by the fact that Hindus, Moslems, Buddhists, Sikhs as well as Jews have accepted exorcism from me as a Christian priest. Quite clearly they acknowledge the cosmic Christ and an Indian Hindu who was a lecturer said he considered Christ as unique and, after exorcism, received baptism.

A South American Hindu asked for baptism after exorcism and an Afghanistan Moslem was baptised and confirmed entirely through exorcism. A Hungarian Jewish psychiatrist, after he had been exorcised, asked to use confession and was later baptised. These people sought the sacraments; I made no attempt to persuade them and I have also exorcised Hindus, Buddhists, Jews, Moslems and Sikhs who did not proceed to baptism but remained in their own religion because I did not want to make it a condition of using exorcism. I am strongly convinced that exorcism, by removing barriers, can be a means whereby people might be brought to Christ spontaneously.

* John 4: 42.
** John 8: 12.

It can clearly be seen from some of the instances in this chapter that exorcism often leads people from paganism into the sacraments of baptism and confirmation. It touches the spring of desire to be different and opens the way to the manifold grace of God. It also brings people from other religions to recognise the power of Christ. This is a particularly interesting fact when people today are treating other religions as equal to Christianity. I have not approached these people; they have approached me. As I have already mentioned, I have been approached by Hindus, Buddhists, Sikhs, Moslems and Jews who have asked me for exorcism and I have undertaken it for them. I am not denying the partial truths of other religions, Hinduism, Buddhism, Mohammedanism and Judaism. On the contrary, it is due to an interest in comparative religion and a recognition that we share the 'one' God that I have been enabled to have a sympathetic understanding of devotees to other religions. I am convinced that in showing willingness to meet their immediate needs without conditions or 'strings attached' they may and do come freely to receive the power of Christ and in so doing the light of the world —Christ—is revealed. The first question of the new Baptism service (1967) is particularly significant. "Do you turn to Christ?" The answer—"I turn to Christ." When the Hindu, the Moslem and Jew said those words at their Baptism they did in fact turn to Christ.

Unfortunately, the Exorcism report seems to assume that people should be prepared for exorcism and baptism within a Christian ecclesiastical structure.* No doubt this may be done in some cases, but today we are faced with a much more fundamental approach, related to the Gospels rather than to the established Church. When people approached Jesus for exorcism, he did it for them as an immediate need and was not concerned as to whether they were Jews or Gentiles. I am sure we should follow his method more directly today. There is a wonderful

* Exorcism Report, p. 24.

opportunity through exorcism to make an "outreach" to those of other religions not purely for dialogue but also to minister to their needs—needs which brought them to seek for the unique power of the living Christ. The approach came from them—each according to their need. The Indian Hindu was conscious of a destructive force intruding on his life. An eastern Moslem, a Sheikh, was conscious of a seductive force trying to lure him. The husband of a Buddhist girl claimed that she was hypnotised by her mentor. A Sikh girl said she was bewitched. A Jewish businessman said he had been cursed and had attempted to get out of a plane on a jet flight.

The saviour of the world

You may well ask why did they not go to ask a minister of their own religion to exorcise them, but each of them said they could not find help or peace within their own religion and sought the power of Christ through his minister to clear them from evil. Here is the most striking evidence of the power of Christ and his cosmic significance for mankind. The need for exorcism is not conditioned by Christian convictions but it applies to those brought up in both Christian and non-Christian cultures, both to Church people and non-Church people alike. In fact we might rightly claim that the need for exorcism is a universal need of mankind. The Hindu whom I mentioned as being baptised later reverted to Hinduism for a time but the evil force returned. The pressure of Hindu relatives tried to draw him. He had to make a renunciation before he was finally cleared. A Moslem woman also reverted to her former religion after she had been baptised and, in the same way, the evil force returned. Again, Moslem friends tried to draw her back. She also had to make a renunciation before the evil force lost hold. As I said previously, a "*δαιμων*" or demon is also translated false deity and if a person comes to the truth about Christ, he should renounce the false deities which intrude on his life. In the same way, as in witchcraft, witches try to pull people back who have left the coven, so adherents to other religions try to pull back their perverts to the old religion. It reminds me of a chorus sung by our Universal Prayer Group of Our Saviour especially for new Christians who come from pagan background: "I am determined to follow Jesus—no turning back, no turning back."

"Jesus Christ is the same yesterday, today and for ever*." Whether it be to a witch or a black magician, an adherent to Buddha or Mohammed, a Jew or a pagan, Christ is finally revealed as "the Way, the Truth and the Life"** for "with authority and power he commandeth the unclean spirits and they come out.†

* Heb. 13: 8.
** John 14: 6.
† Luke 4: 36.

CHAPTER 4

'OVERCOME EVIL WITH GOOD' —RE-CREATION

There is much talk today of a New Age.* What do we mean by new? John Robinson points to the fact that:

> "*there are two Greek words in the New Testament for new, καινος and νεος. Basically νεος refers to novelty, καινος to renewal . . . The new thing that God is doing is always concerned with the re-creation of the old rather than its scrapping and supersession.*"**

Dr. R. D. Laing in his new approach to psychiatry stresses "rebirth—a new kind of ego-functioning, the ego now being the servant of the divine and no longer its betrayer".† This again is a reflection of re-creation. It is the Holy Spirit that is re-creating new men and new women for a New Age.

I have often been struck by the song of the protest marchers "We shall overcome" which seems to me to ring a note of hope for a new sort of creation, or re-creation if you like, when people of all colours and nations will have a new understanding and evil

* The Birth of a New Age Spangler.
** Human Face of God, Robinson, pp. 48, 49.
† Politics of Experience, Laing, pp. 118, 119.

will be overcome by good. When young people talk of good and bad 'vibrations', it is symptomatic of a desire that the good should overcome the bad. Recently two hippies arrived on my doorstep and asked me to bless a ring for them. They told me that it had bad vibrations. I took them into the Church and blessed the ring with holy water and also blessed a crucifix for them to wear as a protection. They said they could perceive good vibrations through the blessing with the sign of the Cross.

The cross—a power today

When I was on the Malcolm Muggeridge "Question Why—Why Evil?" to which I have already referred, I asked John Lennon what he thought was the answer to evil and he quite simply said "The Cross." Now this is profoundly true of many young people today, that they see the significance of the Cross as a symbol of protection against and perhaps even a transforming power over evil. I have sometimes been asked by some young people not purely for exorcism, but baptism, because they needed the protection through being signed with the sign of the Cross. There seems a natural religious instinct to ask for the protection of the sign of the Cross.

For instance, one young man asked me to do an emergency baptism for him because he had become a victim of witchcraft and needed to be saved from their clutches. He was quite convinced that if he had the sign of the Cross on his forehead, he would be safe. The Cross seems to have a special significance for those who have practised or been the victims of witchcraft. One ex-high priest told me his hands would burn, psychically, if he touched a crucifix. Over a period of weeks, I did a number of exorcisms for a witch until the witch-force cleared. Each time I made the sign of the Cross over her near the beginning of the exorcism, she went into unconsciousness and had to be brought round with holy water. Many who call themselves Christians take the Cross too easily for granted and often disregard its significance and power. It is my custom to pray at the altar with outstretched hands in form of a Cross and to use the sign of the Cross on the forehead of those who ask for exorcism. When a Jew enquired about exorcism he asked me whether I could use the Star of David. I explained to him that I must use the Christian symbols as a Christian priest. He finally accepted this because he said Jesus was a Jew. The Cross draws good out of evil and reveals the power of God.

Godspell and Jesus Christ superstar

The musicals "Godspell" and "Jesus Christ Superstar" have often been criticised because they stopped at the Cross and did not go on to the Resurrection. I think people try and write into these musicals what they expect to see instead of accepting them for what they are. Personally, I think they are right to concentrate on the human events of Jesus' life and his sayings, ending in his Cross, because it is just this that is so telling to people who have never seen Jesus in that way before. The knocking of the nails in "Godspell" and the elevation of Jesus on the Cross in "Jesus Christ Superstar" are poignant moments which point to the power of the Cross. It is through seeing Jesus as the Son of Man in the Crucifixion that many come later to recognise him as the Son of God through the Resurrection.

The Jesus Revolution, as Billy Graham called it, is sweeping the U.S.A. "The movement centers in Jesus, these young Christians seem to be possessed with a determination to concentrate entirely on Jesus Christ himself and the fact of His death on the Cross."*

The new Jesus movement

It is in the light of this new emphasis on Jesus that the whole ministry of exorcism should be regarded. Once when I was asked why I did exorcism, I simply answered "Because Jesus did it."

* THE JESUS GENERATION, Graham, p. 13ff.

As I have quoted earlier, Harvey Cox stated "Jesus was viewed by his own age as a great exorcist. His power to cast out demons was central to his ministry." Exorcism should not any longer be regarded as a rite of the Church within an ecclesiastical structure, but as an expression of the Gospel, a part of the new Jesus movement is that His power to cast out demons should again be seen in its true context as an evangelistic means of bringing men and women into His Kingdom, whether hippies or witches, whether black, white, brown or yellow. "I, if I be lifted up, will draw all men unto me."* This is wonderfully demonstrated in "Jesus Christ Superstar" when all those on the stage—coloureds, whites and hippies—turn to look up to Jesus lifted up on the Cross.

Exorcism—Evangelism

A clergyman once said to me that whereas clergy were often shown on TV in protest marches or in a discussion on some controversial subject they were rarely seen functioning as a priest. What amazed him was the publicity on TV and in the Press which I received for a religious activity—exorcism. It is quite true that my TV film of exorcism, televised from my church, produced five hundred letters and I welcomed this as an opportunity to bring—or bring back—the Gospel into the homes and lives of people in ordinary circumstances, many of whom were out of living touch with God. I have had many hundreds of people who have seen me on TV or read about my ministry in press articles request exorcism and it has brought them back into living contact with Jesus through this ministry which I consider it a privilege to use. Some people are not aware how wonderfully the Gospel can be expressed through the modern media on TV and the Press. I have been criticised on the grounds of sensationalism, but I often wonder whether such critics would have considered Jesus

* John 12: 32.

sending devils into swine sensational. They seem to have forgotten that exorcism is part of the Gospel and that the important thing is whether it is true, not whether it is sensational. There is a kind of neo-Pharisaism within the Church today which tries to restrict spiritual activity within conventional rules and seems to forget Jesus saying "Ye have made void the word of God by your tradition."* It is interesting that Simon Tugwell, R.C., expresses the hope that "ministers of the Church would more often use simple exorcisms, remembering the word of God: 'in My name, they will cast out demons'."**

"The Exorcist" shows the way

It is remarkable to some people that a novel entitled THE EXORCIST should be a best-seller in the U.S.A. It is also startling that the film "THE EXORCIST" produced from the novel has had such extraordinary repercussions in the U.S.A. The film has had such a striking impact because people recognise that, unlike Dracula, there is a terrifying truth that lies behind it. Incidentally, the author who is also the producer of the film, William Blatty, told me that it was based on a true story of someone he knew. Both the book and the film contain a profound exposition of the need for exorcism in our modern world. It may seem strange that a girl of eleven should be 'possessed.' It is not really so strange; I have been asked to exorcise a girl of twelve and even one of ten. In each case the parents were convinced that their daughter needed exorcism and also the doctors concerned agreed. When I appeared with the author, on an ITV programme, Eammon Andrews' "Today", in relation to the publication of THE EXORCIST in this country, Eamonn Andrews was amazed at the number of exorcisms (two thousand) I had done in the past four years. Personally, I see these requests as evidence of a revival of spiritual awareness among hundreds of people who have no living connection with any Church.

* Mark 7: 13.
** DID YOU RECEIVE THE SPIRIT, Tugwell, p. 111.

The awareness of evil spirits or forces often brings awareness of the Holy Spirit. The gift of exorcism or 'discernment of spirits' is part of the charismatic movement which is springing up in this country today connected with the Pentecostal movement in the U.S.A. Ling points out "The essential point in Jesus' claim is that his exorcisms are the work of the Spirit of God."* Jesus said himself: "If by the spirit of God, I cast out devils, then the Kingdom of God is come upon you."** The power of the Gospel is again seen through the revival of exorcism. Not only should exorcism be recognised as part of the Jesus movement, but also of the charismatic movement.

Discernment of spirits

One of the astonishing things in the Exorcism Report is that it makes no reference to the charismatic movement at all, nor to the 'discernment of spirits'. Fr. Gilbert Shaw referred to discernment of spirits as a method of diagnosis in exorcism before the recent charismatic movement ever emerged.† It is now even more important because of its link with other gifts of the spirit. There is a fine distinction between 'psychic perceptiveness' and spiritual discernment. There are many people who can sense an atmosphere in a house or in connection with a person, but this is often just a psychic gift, like someone might have a natural gift in the realm of art or music. Spiritual discernment is of a different nature altogether. It is given by God and used under the promptings of the Holy Spirit for a particular spiritual purpose. If it is used for selfish purposes then it is a prostitution of the gift. Personally, through a spiritual experience in retreat, interpreted by the retreat conductor as a 'sign from God', I discovered that the Holy Spirit made me aware of evil in the presence of a person desiring exorcism or spiritual help by a vibration or sensation, (a divine touch if you like), in my hands or head and the movement

* SIGNIFICANCE OF SATAN, Ling, p. 19.
** Mat. 12: 28.
† THE ANGELS OF LIGHT AND THE POWERS OF DARKNESS, p. 81.

of my hands in exorcism reflected the movement of the Holy Spirit. I experienced the same thing when I was exorcised myself by Fr. Gilbert Shaw some years ago and I know two other priests whose hands move in a similar way when they use exorcism. Some people have criticised this as sensational, as if it were some psychic power being used in a dramatic way. Those who have made such criticisms have been those who have never experienced it through themselves. It is a power that comes through the exorcist; it is not something of his own but is given by God. Those who have used it within the context of spiritual discipline under spiritual direction know that it does not lead to spiritual pride, but a deep sense of humility—a wonder that God should use his unworthy servant, for at that moment the exorcist is a servant or instrument of God. When St. Thérèse said that she thanked God for showing her her littleness, it is in that state of soul that a spiritual gift should be used. Unfortunately, priests sometimes show jealousy about spiritual gifts and arguments against such gifts are singularly unconvincing. 'Discerning of spirits' is a gift of the Spirit mentioned by St. Paul* and is also one of the gifts used with the gifts of healing and speaking with tongues in the Pentecostal Movement. It is a great pity that the Pentecostal Movement seems to lay such stress on speaking with tongues almost to the detriment of other spiritual gifts of healing and discerning of spirits. I have met many who have been blessed by the gift of tongues and I would not for one moment wish to decry it, but I am certain that it should be regarded in its true perspective among other gifts and not out of proportion to them.

Baptism of the spirit

The phrase constantly used, baptism in the spirit, by those who are inclined to Pentecostalism is somewhat confusing and tends

* 1 Cor: 12.

to suggest that those who have not received it are only second class Christians. Fr. Simon Tugwell uses the phrase 'discovery of the spirit' instead of 'baptism of the spirit'* and this seems admirably to express the experience which many people, particularly young people, have received in recent years. Michael Harper seems to confine the 'baptism of the spirit' to 'speaking with tongues' instead of recognising that such an experience of the spirit should be seen in a much wider context in relation to a variety of different gifts.

Speaking with tongues

I have sometimes had people who spoke with tongues come to me for exorcism. One man, after he had spoken with tongues, tried to strangle his wife. His ecstatic experience had opened his soul to evil forces and he had to be exorcised. I was told of a priest who committed suicide because he went to a conference where people spoke with tongues and he found himself unable to do so. I came across a woman who had become estranged from her husband who had taken to speaking with tongues because she became afraid of him and his strange moods and tempers. Sometimes, speaking with tongues has tended to be divisive among Christians in a congregation or among families in a household. St. Paul's warning is sometimes easily forgotten, "Though I speak with the tongues of men and of angels and have not love, I am become as sounding brass or a tinkling cymbal."**

Samson Boafe, the founder and spiritual leader of our Universal Prayer Group and a man of great spiritual gifts, prophecy, discernment and healing; took as his text and theme in his last message before leaving England, "Love one another as I have loved you" and asked forgiveness from those he may have hurt, emphasising that love was the supreme gift.

Nevertheless, for some speaking with tongues does bring a quite new release. One striking example was that of a man I was

* DID YOU RECEIVE THE SPIRIT, Tugwell, p. 91.
** 1 Cor. 13: 1.

asked to see who was receiving treatment in a mental hospital. The psychiatrist asked me to see him because he claimed to be possessed. After I had looked into the case carefully, I decided to use exorcism and after I had exorcised him, he suddenly started to sing in tongues; it was as if the Holy Spirit had taken over as the evil spirits departed. He was clearly quite different. It was a release from self, but such a release should culminate in a release for service, otherwise it turns back on itself. A priest who received the gift of tongues needed to express it through spiritual healing before it was seen in perspective.

"Tumi"

One day, I found myself suddenly repeating a word, "tumi," contained within another phrase from a language I did not know. It was at a time when the African group had recently become linked to my Church and I was tentative to minister to them. I asked one of them whether they had come across this word "tumi" and he told me it meant 'spiritual power' in the Ghanaian dialect. This to me was like a Pentecost, they heard me use the word I was given in their own language and it led to a new understanding whereby I was able to use the gifts of the spirit—'healing and discerning of spirits'—for many of them. Previously they had been ministered to by an African, but they desired me to minister to them because they said I understood their spirituality. I was given a new spiritual power—'tumi'—to minister to them. In one case I was also given the gift of prophecy to help one of their leaders. He came to me stating that someone had used an evil force upon him in order to prevent him using concentration for study and he could not study for an important exam. I exorcised him a few times and his concentration returned. I felt inspired to tell him at the time of the exorcism that it had been revealed to me that he would pass his exam because it was part of God's plan for him. In spite of strong fears to the contrary, he passed his exams and later became a qualified barrister. He also developed a new gift of spiritual healing at the same time.

It is sometimes said that speaking in tongues comes through someone who has himself received the gift laying his hands on you, but this is not necessarily so. It may come almost out of the blue and the person may not even realise what he is doing. It may come in a time of prayer similar to an ecstasy or it may be that this particular spiritual gift is not for you. I firmly believe that the laying on of hands brings spiritual blessings and gifts, but who are we to say what gifts may be bestowed by this means. I remember laying my hands on a priest in exorcism who later developed the gift of discerning of spirits himself. I also laid my hands on a woman through exorcism and one day she suddenly discovered a gift of the spirit through exorcising her daughter in a moment of inspiration. After I had laid my hands on another priest, he developed an entirely new gift of healing. I know two women who each earnestly desired the gift of healing and asked a priest to lay hands on her. One woman felt a tingling in the throat and the other a touch on the tongue. Neither developed the gift of tongues but each had received a gift of healing. I think it is extremely important that we should not as ministers or people have preconceived notions of the way in which the Spirit may work on or in us. We should not assume that others will have the same experience as ourselves—it is a grave mistake which causes many misgivings. If we give or receive the laying on of hands let God use us as His servants in His way and not in ours. Newman once said that "we only become ourselves when we lose sight of ourselves" and Thomas Merton said that "we only become ourselves when we cease trying to become what we always wanted to be." The 'gift of tongues' particularly and also other 'gifts of the spirit' bring a release from self and it is this which is a re-creation of the soul or personality. For some this may mean a breakdown which will be a sort of spiritual breakthrough, a need for penitence and a recognition of our dependence upon God. Unless a person is prepared to be re-orientated towards God, re-created by his Spirit and through his grace, he will fail to be a true servant of God.

Jesus in the wilderness

Jesus went through the temptations in the wilderness after he had been baptised by John the Baptist and received the Holy Spirit in his baptism.

Harry Williams emphasises this point when he says that:

> "*it is by the Spirit that Jesus is driven, thrown out is the actual word, into the wilderness, the same Spirit which had brought Him the conviction of being called to do great things . . . The story of Jesus reminds us that being thrown out in this way must be an inevitable concomitant of our call to God's service.*"*

And so we will have to face similar temptations, and if we have received the Spirit, the temptations may be greater, not less. Harry Williams goes on to say:

> "*We are tempted of Satan. Tempted to give up, to despair. Tempted to cynicism. Tempted sometimes to cruelty. Tempted not to help others when we know we can . . . and behind each and all these temptations is the temptation to disbelieve what we are, the temptation to distrust ourselves.*"*

Make stones bread

It is the first temptation of Jesus to 'make stones bread' which is a challenge to us, to our own inadequacy, to our own incapacity, to our own inability to recognise that we have no power of ourselves to help ourselves, but our 'sufficiency is of God'. In fact it is a temptation to self-pity engendered by self-love. St. Augustine points to the two loves; the one that despises self for the love of God and the other, the love of self to the despising of God.** The true servant of God must be wholly dependent upon God, not his own resources. Whether he belittles or exalts himself,

* TRUE WILDERNESS, Williams, pp. 32, 33.
** St Augustine, Civitate Dei XIV 28.

whether it is self pity or self love, he must be surrendered to God. If we are called to fast or other forms of self-denial it is a test of our willingness, a test as to whether we are willing to give ourselves in love to God.

All this power

The second temptation of Jesus is that of self-will. "All this power will I give thee." It is a challenge to our own self-possession, our desire to get our own way and to go our own way often through a ruthless suppression of or disregard for others. The danger of using powers to control others is that of the magician or the witch. The true servant of God must learn self-discipline and surrender, for a man's strong point is his danger point and should be dedicated to God.

Cast thyself down

The third temptation of Jesus is that of self-expression: "Cast thyself down." It is a challenge to our ambition, to show others what we can do—a desire for self-advertisement. The danger with all gifts is to use them as a means of self-expression. Many people have gifts of healing, seeking out others to experiment or try out their gifts—thus using them not for the glory of God or the needs of others, but purely as a means of self-expression. The true servant of God is called or used by God to heal or help others regardless of his own desire and even sometimes in spite of his own reluctance to do so.

Temptation not oppression

It is important to point out that temptation is quite distinct from diabolical oppression. In temptation, the devil attacks from outside like he did to Jesus, but in oppression or possession he has gained a hold on the persons (he has become attached to the aura if you like). Sometimes a person goes through a period of darkness in which he is severely tempted because it brings a new detachment from self. As Dr. Ramsey says: "The darkness is apposite. The self is being negated. It is a real dying to self."*

The dark night

It is this darkness to which St. John of the Cross refers as the "dark night of the sense" in his famous treatise "The Dark Night of the Soul". "The night of the sense is common and comes to many."

It is often assumed that St. John of the Cross wrote for monks and nuns and the spiritually advanced. However, Dr. Mascall asserts that this is a mistaken notion and that St. John of the Cross himself says that he wrote that "all, whether beginners or proficients may know how to commit themselves to God's guidance".** The 'dark night of the sense'—the purging of all the senses from selfish desire—can be compared to the wilderness. As St. John of the Cross himself explains the reason for the dark night of the sense when he says that 'God sets the soul in this dark night to the end He may quench and purge its sensual desire'.†

Contemplation rediscovered

Now it is interesting to find that Simon Tugwell describes what the neo-Pentecostals think of as "baptism in the spirit" as a "touch of infused contemplation".†† He goes on to point out that baptism in the spirit, far from being the gift of entire sanctification, is a kind of initiatory experience of the Holy Spirit, a beginning of contemplation. He links the charismatic gifts and contemplation by saying:

> "*The beginning of contemplation is the conscious coming into play of the gifts of the spirit bestowed in principle at baptism but only now beginning to exercise their proper role in actual life and experience.*"‡

* SACRED AND SECULAR, Ramsey, p. 39.
** A GUIDE TO MOUNT CARMEL, Mascall, pp. 10, 11, 12.
† PEER'S TRANSLATION, p. 371.
†† DID YOU RECEIVE THE SPIRIT, Tugwell, p. 91.
‡ DID YOU RECEIVE THE SPIRIT, Tugwell, Chap. III, p. 29ff.

Now, I am quite convinced that some of those who call themselves agnostics, those who retain reverence for the things of God and yet have lost the reality, are passing through the dark night of the sense without realising it. I know an intelligent agnostic with a strong sense of the sacred who found it difficult to experience reality in worship. However, when he realised that the writings of St. John of the Cross applied to his condition, he found a new experience in prayer—a veritable discovery of the Holy Spirit.

In the past, it has so easily been assumed that contemplation is purely for monks and nuns that it was not thought possible for married people living in the world. Dr. Ramsey has pointed out that "contemplation, desiring God and enjoying glimpses of God—that is something for all".* He goes on to say that "there are signs of a new discovery of contemplative prayer in the setting of everyday life. May it be the prayer which can reach from the religious to the religionless?" I well remember a former Carmelite nun coming to me for spiritual advice. She had by that time left the convent through ill health, become an Anglican, married and had two children. She told me that in spite of the fact that she had practised the contemplative life for some years in a Carmelite convent, she had lost all taste for prayer and was in spiritual misery through ill informed direction of a number of priests. She was clearly suffering from a spiritual oppression and under demonic attack. After I exorcised her and she received the sacraments, she rediscovered the grace of contemplation and was on one occasion able to do a night vigil in front of the sacrament and also look after her children during the day.

God through us is not "God in us"

It is as well to remember that Jesus suffered the Temptations in the Wilderness after he had received the Holy Spirit in his

* RETREATS TODAY by Dr. Ramsey, p. 17.

baptism. If we have received a new 'discovery of the Holy Spirit,' (or 'baptism in the Spirit'—if you like), there will be many parts of our soul which need purifying and cleansing and this may take years. We must distinguish between God's work in us and God's work through us to others. We need not wait until we are saints because God's grace can work through us in spite of ourselves because it is his power and not our own. However, we must not give way to the pride of thinking we are far advanced when we may only be near the beginning. Dr. Pusey once said that when he was a young man he spent a lot of time trying to convert others but as he grew older he realised how much he himself needed converting. Yet contemplation culminates in action and the true servant of God should fulfil the role of 'God's man for others' in the power of the Holy Spirit, not his own.

Jesus' mission

It is in this connection that I want to investigate Jesus' own interpretation of his mission when he took up the book of Isaiah in the synagogue at Nazareth and read:

> "*The Spirit of the Lord is upon me, because he hath anointed me to preach the gospel to the poor; he hath sent me to heal the broken hearted, to preach deliverance to the captives and recovering of sight to the blind, to set at liberty them that are bruised.*"*

Then Jesus said "This day is the scripture fulfilled in your ears".*

Jesus interpreted his own Mission in terms of the Servant of Isaiah. Furthermore he says "the Son of Man came not to be ministered unto but to minister and to give his life a ransom for many".* Clearly he sees himself not purely in the role of the Servant but as the Suffering Servant.

This anointing of Jesus was a secret spiritual anointing in

* Luke 4: 17, 18, quote from Isaiah 61: 1.

contrast to his Baptism. The anointing of the Holy Spirit was for a special mission to preach, to heal and to liberate or deliver from evil, (exorcise.) So those who are called to be his ministers must see themselves in the role of the Servant or Suffering Servant. So, they will receive the 'gifts of the spirit' in the form of spiritual anointing like touches of infused contemplation, 'they are in fact the most secret and delicate anointings of the Holy Spirit'* Christ coming from *Χριστος* means the 'anointed one' and those who are called to be his ministers and servants of God will receive what Teilhard de Charden describes as a 'christification'. The charismatic Christ links the Jesus movement with the charismatic movement because Jesus Christ was anointed by the Holy Spirit.

Prophecy and preaching

When we turn to preaching, it is natural to turn to 'speaking with tongues', but preaching should really be connected with the 'gift of prophecy' St. Paul was faced with a similar situation in the Corinthian Church as we find today in relation to 'speaking with tongues'. He said quite specifically: "He that speaketh in an unknown tongue edifieth himself, but he that prophesieth edifieth the Church." Clearly, he shows that 'speaking with tongues' is better used as a private devotion and not intended for public worship. It is an interesting fact that in our Universal Prayer Group, there have been numerous occasions when members have spoken in tongues and passed through trance experiences, but the African leaders explained to me that they tended to restrain such activities even if they occur spontaneously because they disturb and sometimes even frighten other members of the Group, just as St. Paul did in the Corinthian Church. One of the African Pentecostal ministers said to me that the Pentecostal movement emphasised all the ninefold gifts of the spirit** and some of the English seemed to have got the 'speaking with tongues' out of

* LIVING FLAME OF LOVE, Stanza III, 36, 38, 39.
** 1 Cor. 12.

proportion. The African leaders use the interpretation of dreams rather than tongues because they believe that important revelations are given in dreams through the unconscious, whereas the gift of tongues is often consciously cultivated after the primary experience.

I am sure the English can learn a great deal about the use of these gifts from the African and Asian countries. They seem to forget that trance experiences are more natural to African or Asian people than to English.

Men who discern

Let us return to the gift of prophecy and preaching. As Professor C. H. Dodd once said: "Foresight was primarily insight and prediction the dramatisation of spiritual judgement." The prophets were men who applied essential principles of revelation to new situations and 'brought forth new truth from the depths of their inspired insights'.* There are men who discern the signs of the times. It is in this sense, no doubt, that Canon Roger Lloyd describes both John Robinson and Harry Williams as modern prophets.

New preaching

During the Honest to God debate, I asked John Robinson to come and preach at a Lent Course; he replied by suggesting a Dialogue in which I posed the questions. I readily agreed and it proved most valuable and had a spontaneity about it which people thought was most inspiring. We seem to forget that Jesus' parable of the Good Samaritan arose out of a dialogue with a lawyer who asked "Who is my neighbour?" The great saying of Jesus—"I am the Way, the Truth and the Life,"—was stated in answer to a question from his disciple Thomas, "How can we know the way?" It is not possible that the dialogue as a means of communication may reveal the truths of the Gospel,

* See Skinner, PROPHECY AND RELIGION, p. 3.

like Jesus' dialogues in the Gospels, in a way which a prepared manuscript does not?

In the same way "Jesus Christ Superstar" presents a challenge in the form of a question, in contrast to Oberammergau in traditional forms. 'Jesus Christ Superstar, Do you think you're what they say you are?' The late Professor Raven once said that the time has now ceased when people want to hear read what they could equally well read for themselves. I was amazed, after I was interviewed for a TV programme and the questions were later cut out, how well the answers hung together. I felt it was inspired by the spontaneity of the moment and I was actually surprised by what I said. I could not help thinking that it was far better than what I would have said if I had prepared a manuscript.

Preaching and the Spirit

Nevertheless, I am far from denying the more ordinary form of preaching. Personally, I consider that preaching is totally different from a lecture because preaching depends upon the spiritual response of the congregation. I find that some congregations seem almost to emanate a kind of resistance, while with others one can have the sensation of the Spirit and feel moved through their response. I have been conscious of saying things I never intended and knowing that 'it is not you that speak, but the Holy Spirit'. People have sometimes referred to things which have been said which I have forgotten because they were not part of my thought at all. Professor Raven talks of the preacher:

> "*He is to impart the sharing of the Spirit—not a discourse about God but a means of bringing God to the people . . . When he and they have been in real sympathy, then, though the speech may have been halting, technically poor and liable to hostile comment, the intention of it will not have been lost; the experience too big for words will have been shared; the conviction will have been communicated.*"*

* CREATOR SPIRIT, Raven, pp. 173, 175.

I was once told as a young man never to deflect from a manuscript; now I know that this would block the Holy Spirit, for we preach not ourselves but Christ Jesus our Lord. In the Old Testament, the prophet spoke to the individual, (like Elijah to Ahab), or to the nation, (like Isaiah). The gift of prophecy may be given for private counselling or for public preaching, and essentially depends on revelation in contrast to reason. The New Theology with its emphasis on 'new truth' opens the way to the New Spirituality. The 'New Spirituality' as I see it lays emphasis on God's gifts rather than man's efforts. It points the way to contemplation and mysticism rather than meditation and asceticism; it stresses the receiving of the gifts of the Spirit rather than the acquiring of virtues and the importance of overcoming of evil rather than salvation from sin.

Alongside the gift of prophecy, there comes naturally the gifts of knowledge, and wisdom-revealed knowledge, and wisdom, not that which comes from reason. Fr. Gilbert Shaw said he once had a spiritual experience which made him feel he was 'going mad'. He later interpreted it in terms of the 'crown of thorns', the white martyrdom—bearing witness for the truth in the face of opposition.

The interview is spiritual

Now surely this is the gift of knowledge and wisdom given by God for spiritual counselling—to preach deliverance—that through spiritual knowledge a new release and liberation may come. In the Billy Graham Crusade, preaching was followed up by spiritual counselling. However, in a spiritual way, some may be given a special gift of knowledge so that when interviewing someone a special knowledge is revealed about the person who sometimes says "How did you know?" It is not guess work like the psychic, (with or without the crystal)—it is exact knowledge given for a special spiritual purpose to guide, direct or counsel them when they might not have divulged something themselves.

It is extremely interesting to find John Robinson saying

"My own experience is that I am really praying for people agonising with God for them, precisely as I meet them and really give my soul to them."* He also says that intercession "may consist simply in listening, when we take the otherness of the other person most seriously." Again he says "Prayer is the responsibility to meet others, with all that I have . . . to expect to meet God in the way." Now it seems to me that what John Robinson calls prayer, I would describe as a spiritual interview, giving my soul to the person, an extension of prayer for them in which spiritual knowledge is revealed. If someone has turned up on the doorstep suddenly, I have not been able to pray for them beforehand, yet spiritual knowledge has still been revealed concerning them in an interview.

Theology is spiritual

It is in this way that the New Theology leads naturally to the New Spirituality. I have found the recent writings of John Robinson and Harry Williams strangely fascinating because they relate the academic study of Theology to personal relationships and personal experience. No doubt this is the reason why they have aroused a far wider interest among many people outside the sphere of academic Theology. John Robinson has identified himself with agnostics and atheists and Harry Williams has attempted to identify himself with the mentally afflicted. In so doing they have emphasised the relevance for the parish priest of identifying himself with his people in their intellectual doubts and neurotic conditions.

John Robinson considers the need of today is an 'answering Theology' which takes place between the Church and the world over living issues. He has made Theology 'come alive' for those who have never thought about it. Harry Williams talks of a 'theology of the self' and reveals interior states of soul often found amidst the tensions of the modern world. He makes spirituality

* Honest to God, Robinson, p. 100.

'come alive' for those who have never recognised the need of it. Dr. Eric Mascall has recently pointed to the sheer pastoral necessity for a 'Theology of Exorcism' and the Exorcism Report has presented a challenge for people to recognise the reality of evil in our midst.

Personally it seems to me that what is also badly needed is a 'Theology of the Spiritual Life' so that we can understand the ways of the Spirit and within that framework the discernment of spirits and exorcism naturally fit.

New ways of the spirit

If we are to regard things existentially, then the New Spirituality springs from experience of the Holy Spirit. It is interesting to find a sixth former who had experienced spiritual healing claiming that his Religious Education teacher was obscuring the spiritual significance of the miracles by explaining them in psychological terms. It was also interesting to hear a teenager describe how he had seen his father just after his death, when his housemaster had just said that he did not acknowledge departed spirits.

I have recently visited a number of schools and spoken to voluntary societies. On two separate occasions when they expected thirty to forty teenagers, two hundred to three hundred came. Admittedly, ghosts and witches are an unusual subject, but it is not purely a psychic interest that attracts young people. Some of them asked me about meditation and prayer in the most open way. In fact it was some of the questions that came from the staff which reflected doubt and materialism, rather than those which came from the boys and girls. It seems that the Jesus generation, as it is sometimes called, is far more concerned with spirituality than those of ten or twenty years ago. The present young generation often feel that the Church has failed to meet spiritual needs and have sought meditation elsewhere. This tendency to reach beyond materialism through meditation is reflected in George Harrison's song "Within you, without you?"—

"We were talking—about the love that's gone so cold and the people who gain the world and lose their soul—they don't know—they can't see—are you one of them? When you've seen beyond yourself—then you may find peace of mind."

The spirit and young people

It is a curious fact that the Times Review of one of my broadcasts on exorcism was entitled "Seeing Beyond" and criticised a psychiatrist on the programme for failing to recognise such a need. Surely it is just this, seeing beyond, which many young people are finding through psychic experience. That is why young people become irritated with the attitude of those who try to project psychological and sociological ideas of the 20th century into the stories of the New Testament. Professor Raven once said that it was presumptuous to assume that the miracles could not happen, because it was the task of Theology to explain the miracles, not to explain them away!*

It is this prevalent interest in mysticism and the things of the spirit which has had its influence both inside and outside the Church. There has not only been a reaction against the scientific mode of thinking by young people outside the Church and a turning to meditation, but also a reaction against the formal rites and ceremonies within the Church and a turning to the gifts of the Spirit. Spiritual gifts are not purely those of 'speaking with tongues' or 'healing', but 'knowledge' and 'wisdom'. It is this gift which gives an insight into a person's problem which cannot be done in a healing service or by spiritual administration alone.

Healing of the memories

It is sometimes not recognised that something more is needed than anointing or laying on of hands, even when combined with confession, to make a person whole. It is not purely suffering or sin but other factors which are inhibiting a person's soul. It is the healing of the memories which is really needed. It is not purely

* Experience and Interpretation, Raven, p. 78.

contained in the question "What's wrong with you?" or "What have you done wrong?", but "When were you unhappy or sad?" Christ was anointed not purely to heal the sick, but the broken hearted.

When I have undertaken the healing of the memories, I have used the laying-on of hands with the person seated and relaxed, starting with the prayer "Almighty God unto whom all hearts be open, all desires known and from whom no secrets are hid, cleanse the thoughts of our hearts by the inspiration of thy Holy Spirit", etc., and then taking them through rather painful memories that they may see them in the light of God and ending with the "Peace of God which passeth all understanding." Agnes Sanford refers to the "Healing of the Memories" as "unconscious speaking to unconscious."*

One man I ministered to had been having suicidal tendencies. I had exorcised and anointed him and he had also received absolution. Then I took him back through the healing of the memories to the suicide of his wife when he could smell the smell of gas and it was the healing of this memory in the light of God which finally gave him peace.

Another example was that of a man who had been in prison years before, charged with homosexual offences, and sacked from his firm for stealing. He had haunting fears of being arrested although he was now quite innocent. He also feared that his marriage might break up or he might lose his job. I took him back to these memories and the surrounding circumstances under the guidance of the Holy Spirit and gave him new hope.

There was also a person who had a sex change and needed healing of the memories. Starting life as a boy, there were many painful memories and later an operation was performed after he had been married for some years. I took her back through these memories in the light of Christ, which gave her a sense of release from the unhappy past.

* GIFTS OF THE SPIRIT, Sanford.

Another woman recalled an unhappy childhood through witchcraft which had been practised by her relatives. She had been a victim of the 'left hand path' and used the left hand more than the right. When she had been exorcised and anointed and finally received the healing of the memories, she found a new balance of use in her right hand. She quite literally 'came right' so to speak and found the use of her right hand in ways she had never used it in her life before.

There was a young American girl who flew to London to see me because she had been haunted by the memories of her father and brother, both of whom had died tragically. She needed exorcism for drawing away their spirits, but most of all healing of the memories which gave her a new peace not found at all through psychiatry.

There was also a young girl who had a number of unhappy affairs and also needed healing of the memories. She identified herself with Mary Magdalene and said how much she liked the song of Mary Magdalene in Jesus Christ Superstar, "I don't know how to love him".

It is not often realised that Jesus Christ himself took the Woman of Samaria through the healing of the memories when he told her of her association with seven men and brought her to understand the truth about God.

Jesus Christ did not merely bring deliverance to or heal people, but made them whole. People are delivered from evil in order that their lives may be re-created in the service of God.

New ways of the spirit

Quite clearly, the Holy Spirit is guiding us in this Day and Age to discover new ways of preaching, healing and deliverance. Preaching or communication of the Gospel is seen through dialogue and even drama. Healing is found through healing of the memories as well as a much wider use of healing gifts through the hands. Deliverance is achieved through discernment of spirits and binding of evil forces, not purely through ritualistic rites. A new discovery of the Holy Spirit in prayer, through speaking in tongues or supplication in the Spirit and a renewal of contemplation and mysticism has also emerged in recent years.

Not an evil age—a new age

Although some appear to call it an 'evil age', others refer to a 'new age'. After all, we have the New English Bible, the New Liturgy, the New Theology and the New Spirituality. This New Spirituality or new ways of the Holy Spirit is expressed in a new spontaneity, simplicity and sincerity. People are not so hidebound by tradition and are open to new ways. An awareness of evil forces and evil spirits and sensitivity to evil brings new spiritual awareness of God and His Holy Spirit.

Whereas, in the 'sixties', there was a tendency to obscure the supernatural, now in the 'seventies' there is a wind of change through the widespread interest in the psychic which leads beyond the rational to the spiritual. This is reflected in Carl Jung's prophetic words on his eighty-fifth birthday: "There is a deep need in the world just now for spiritual guidance, almost any kind of spiritual guidance."* This is profoundly true today and he was looking far ahead, for there has been a marked reaction against the scientific mode of thinking which makes young people today almost regard those who call themselves 'agnostic' as being 'square', not because they deny the spiritual but because they decry the psychic.

Many young people are searching for leadership in spiritual things and many meditation societies and 'awareness' groups have been formed. Young people tend to think more in terms of 'awareness' rather than 'apprehension' and 'percept' is more important than 'concept.'

The cure of souls in the seventies

In a strange way, the doubts of the sixties have been replaced by the needs of the seventies and the recognition of Christ as seen

* Article, Art of Living, Sunday Times, July 17th, 1960.

in "Jesus Christ Superstar" and "Godspell" has filled the popular mind in place of the 'God is Dead' phraseology. In a strange and wonderful way, the power of the Gospel is being revealed again through people turning to God in times of need. They experience the power of Christ through healing and exorcism. Hence the term 'cure of the souls' used at the Institution of a new Vicar has again become particularly relevant through the demands for healing of mind, body and spirit. Instead of clergy spending their time organising protest marches or housing associations, they should remember the threefold commission of Christ to preach, —if necessary through dialogue—to heal—if necessary of the memories—and to bring deliverance, if necessary through exorcism. It is in this way that the 'cure of souls' has a new significance of meaning and people are met at the point of their need. How often have I asked people who have been to see me from different parts of England whether they have seen a local priest or minister. Sadly, time and time again I have been told that they have seen a local priest but he neither could nor would undertake healing or deliverance for them nor even discuss their problems with them. I am not altogether blaming them. Many ministers are victims of a system which is blissfully unaware of the new spiritual needs and sometimes rather reluctant to use the means of spiritual help or of communication already available.

No doubt it can be argued that healing and deliverance are specialist ministries and that is to a certain extent true through the gifts of the Spirit. However, the charismatic movement is becoming more widespread and more and more priests and ministers are becoming awakened to the power of the Holy Spirit in new ways. The sad thing is that so many people are seeking spiritual help even in meditation as well as healing elsewhere because so often priests and ministers are not prepared to give it. Actually the Samaritans have been very helpful and have sent me certain cases where they considered exorcism is needed. I have, in the same way, sent certain people to them who needed 'befriending'.

The priest is needed

There were certain TV programmes and press articles in the sixties tending to suggest that the role of the priest is being largely taken over by psychiatrists and social workers. It has even been suggested that a priest should be qualified in some profession other than his own. In contrast, the demands for exorcism in the present age make it abundantly clear that the role of the priest is more than ever needed. Exorcism needs professional skill and it is very difficult for a layman or laywoman to undertake it because it is often involved with sacraments. Here is a wonderful opportunity for a priest or minister to come into his own in a sphere quite distinct from psychiatrists or social workers. Psychiatrists and social workers recognise this by sending people to priests for exorcism when they would not do so for other things. No doubt it can be argued that not all priests can or should do exorcisms. However, it is necessary to differentiate between major and minor exorcisms. In minor exorcisms where a person has been involved in or under an evil influence, any priest should be able to bind such influence by saying "I bind all evil forces coming through, from or surrounding a certain person or cult," and bless the person either with the sign of the Cross or with the laying on of hands. This is done with the authority of Christ through his Church and does not demand any special spiritual gift.

Major exorcism—A specialist job

On the other hand, major exorcisms where violent or seductive forces are involved and the person may be under legal or medical supervision should be left to the experienced exorcist. In any doubt, a priest should consult an exorcist known to the Diocese who can advise on such matters.

When I was asked at a Conference to speak about the Minister's or Priest's Spirituality, I pointed out that some priests who practised exorcism had left the ministry and the monastery and marriages had been broken up too. The Devil is always intent on destroying priests. The Roman Rituals is wise in asserting that the qualities required in an exorcist are 'prudence, piety and moral integrity'. If a priest is going to act as an exorcist in a specialist ministry he must recognise the dangers—the chinks in his armour which are hate, fear, doubt and illicit sex—otherwise he may play literally into the hands of the devil and the forces he is trying to destroy may end in destroying him. It means for such a priest a re-orientation of his whole spiritual life to be readily available to meet spiritual needs in crises. Francoise Strachan asserts that an exorcist should have nerves of steel*—perhaps she is right. However, a priest must never be too proud to recognise when he may need an exorcism or healing himself. There was a remarkable unanimity between an evangelical minister who also spoke on the Minister's Spirituality at the Conference and myself in both acknowledging the need of confession and dependence upon the gifts of the Holy Spirit. Dr. Ramsey strongly emphasises this in one of his Ordination charges.

> *"If you use sacramental confession do not slip out of it. If you do not use sacramental confession, ask yourself if it would not be a good thing that you should."***

Exorcism—A gift

Some priests are very critical of those who use the gifts of the Spirit because they consider they are proud, but it is often a disguise for jealousy. As Dr. Ramsey (Ordination Charges) points out: "You can be jealous of a man because he has gifts you would like." Let us remember that a mere following of the ritualistic rite and rubrics is not enough because the exorcisms of Jesus 'were of the Holy Spirit.' A priest who purely uses the rite is not always open to the inspiration of the Holy Spirit and often too self-conceited to admit it. He may know all the techniques and yet not be guided by the Holy Spirit at all.

* CASTING OUT THE DEVILS, Strachan, p. 18.
** THE CHRISTIAN PRIEST TODAY, Ramsey, p. 71.

The life of an exorcist

A priest who is genuinely used by the Holy Spirit is aware of a power which is not his own. It is often when he is overtired or reluctant to undertake exorcism that the Holy Spirit works mightily upon the person regardless of himself. Fr. Gilbert Shaw stressed penitence and dependence to fulfil such a ministry and it is vital for every priest to recognise that he should be able to act as a spiritual director or counsellor as well as an exorcist and that exorcism should be seen within the framework of spirituality and not in isolation from it. I was once asked by an interviewer whether I was obsessed by exorcism. I replied by stating that I was bored by it because I was really interested in spirituality, not evil. It has been held that priests who practise exorcism should read and learn about witchcraft. I do not myself believe that this is at all wise, as such reading could produce a stimulation to become involved in it. Those witches who come to a priest are at the point of rejecting it and they want his spiritual help. It is spirituality that the priest needs to know about—ways of spiritual direction, not witchcraft. Some priests are sadly lacking in this respect and have little understanding of spirituality.

Exorcist's discipline

In traditional spirituality, there has been a secret discipline for exorcists of fasting and in some cases of self-scourging. Priests who ignore these disciplines do so at their peril, but they should only be used under spiritual direction to avoid the pitfalls of spiritual pride. For fasting is identification with Jesus in the Wilderness and self-scourging identification with Jesus in his passion. It is not masochism as some psychiatrists might call it, because it gives no pleasure but only spiritual strength to those who practise it. Von Hugel says: "Souls exist which are truly called to such mortifications. Yet it is Love, God, that first should be in our hearts; and if that Love impels us to such deeds, we will attempt to do them."* Now I know a priest who discovered that

* THE LIFE OF PRAYER, Hugel, p. 60.

two of his flock were having an illicit affair and although he remonstrated with them, it was of no avail. Wherefore, as an act of loving desire to God for them, he resolved to scourge himself every day in Lent for them. The affair was broken by penitence and confession in Holy Week and relationships transformed at the altar on Easter Day. A member of a P.C.C. walked out of a meeting and resigned and the parish priest undertook a special fast for him and met him in the street during the fast. The man apologised and unexpectedly withdrew his resignation. These examples show quite clearly that if we identify ourselves with Jesus in this way, he can use us, and so it seems quite natural to use such disciplines within the ministry of exorcism.

The Pope's title 'servant of the servants of God' applies also to the simple priest who is inspired by the Suffering Servant, 'by his stripes we are healed'. The priest who is truly 'God's man for others', and who bears the people on his heart should put up the text on his desk: 'For their sakes, I dedicate myself'. Francoise Strachan says: "One of the main reasons why there are so few good exorcists about is that the work is exceptionally hard and one must be utterly dedicated in one's intention."*

The priest and God

It is dedication for others' sakes without selfish ambition or safety precautions. It may mean risking his reputation or health, which others carefully preserve, but it is following Jesus and caring for souls rather than synods. His prayer will be an offering to God in contemplation, a 'deepening longing for God' as Dr. Ramsey calls it, in contrast to 'meditation—something that is very easily twisted into reflection upon our own mental processes and ideas'. There is a widespread interest in meditation of various kinds at the moment, some quite unrelated to God, so it is all the more important for the priest to contemplate God.

Contemplation leads us through adoration to intercession,

* Casting out the Devils, Strachan, p. 18.

but divinely directed intercession in which God shows us for whom he desires us to pray. St. John of the Cross puts it:

"*If God desires to receive a prayer for that person, he will move his will and give him a desire to pray for him; if God desires not such prayer, that other person will not be able nor will desire to pray, though he make great efforts to do so; at times God will cause him to pray for others of whom he has never heard.*"*

On one occasion I saw a girl in prayer whom I had never seen before, but she subsequently appeared on my doorstep and if I had not seen her in prayer beforehand, I would not have known what she needed.

The truth about evil

Recently, I was asked to give a talk to clergy and others on the Reality of Evil, not just Exorcism, and I was glad to do so because I think there is a great deal of confusion about evil. Dr. Temple distinguished three forms of evil, 'Intellectual Evil or Error, Emotional Evil or suffering, Moral Evil or Sin'.** Dr. Temple also says:

"*Shelve the responsibility for human evil on to Satan if you will; personally I believe he exists and a large share of that responsibility belongs to him and his subordinate evil spirits.*"†

One man wrote to me and said that evil is all in the mind, ignoring other forms of evil.

Another clergyman who has dealt with departed spirits said he had never come across an 'evil spirit', refusing to accept anything outside his own preconceived ideas. Neither of these people are facing the stark reality of evil. We only have to recall the concentration camps and gas chambers of Hitler to recognise the reality of evil. As St. Augustine once put it, "God judged it better to bring good out of evil than to suffer no evil to exist."††

* Ascent of Mount Carmel, Bk. III, Ch. II, p. 230, Peers' translation.
** Mens Creatrix, Temple, p. 273.
† Nature, Man and God, Temple, p. 503.
†† St. Augustine, Enchirid XXVII.

A woman, after she had been exorcised by me, told me how a clergyman tried to convince her she was not 'evil' but she told him quite bluntly that she knew there was evil in her and I had not suggested it. She came for a second exorcism in spite of his rather naive comments and was entirely cleared of an evil oppression. It does not help people to tell them they are not evil when they know there is evil in them or on them. In contrast they find a great relief when someone believes that what they say is true and deals with it. Personally, I do not believe in talking about evil people unless a person has dedicated themselves to evil, and has therefore been overcome by evil. In most cases, it is easier to describe the situation by saying that evil is on or in a person because evil has an objective reality apart from the person. Some people rather naively assume that I think all evil is demonic. Naturally there is evil emanating from human self-will and human wills are no less responsible because they are allied to the demonic. If good emanates from God, then it is reasonable to assume that evil is induced by Satan who distorts men's minds and falsifies their judgements, but that does not alter the fact in the very least that man has free will to rebel against God, as in the Genesis story of Adam. Although Adam (Man) was tempted by the serpent (Satan) he sinned of his own free will.*

Thou hast no power

Of course, there are some who are afraid of evil and tend to exaggerate it. One woman described two women she worked with as 'witches'. No doubt, they may have been jealous or unkind, but there was not the slightest evidence of witchcraft. Another woman convinced herself that no-one could overcome an evil telepathy which was being exerted on her. I had to explain in both cases in the words of Jesus to Pilate: "Thou hast no power at all against me." No one, no witch nor black magician, has any powers whatever against the power of God if people turn to God. People often talk of white magic and put up white crosses or

* Gen: 3.

pentagrams as a defence, but they do not realise that black magic is often more powerful than white magic and overcomes it. Francoise Strachan says "Faith in the indwelling power of God is the shield of protection."* The defence against evil and Satanic powers is the power of prayer and the use of the crucifix and holy water and if necessary exorcism. Black magic may defeat white magic, but the Holy Spirit breaks up black magic entirely. I have had white witches ask me for help with exorcism when black forces have been used because they know the power of God can defeat them. They realise that white magic has not got the same power.

Many thousands of good people

Some people may be worried by what has been said about evil in this book, but they can rest assured that there are many thousands of good people who have never been involved in this sort of evil and will never need exorcism because their innocence has never been destroyed. Thank God. There have been many good people who pray and worship regularly yet have never used private confession in the Church of England. Some have even said that they never realised it was available because their particular Church may not have mentioned it. In the same way, many people have never thought of such a thing as exorcism. Exorcism is used for drawing away departed spirits (who are undetached, not necessarily evil), as well as driving away evil spirits. In the same way as Confession is widely used by people who are not in mortal sin, exorcism is coming to be more widely used by people who feel oppressed yet not possessed.

Evil—hate—good—love

Another young man described a strange feeling 'coming over' him which made him hate other people. A diplomat's wife told me of a strange experience she had in a European country where a

* CASTING OUT DEVILS, Strachan, p. 18.

child to whom she refused help put an 'evil eye' on her. We seem to forget that Jesus referred to this when he said "If thine eye be evil, thy whole body will be full of darkness."* The 'evil eye' is an expression of hate. In the same way an African girl said she saw in a dream her half sister put an evil spell on her through hate. One priest who did a lot of healing and exorcism once said that if a person becomes bitter, he never really becomes better. Bitterness feeds on hate. When we consider the conflict between God and Satan or between good and evil, it is interesting to find Harry Williams interpreting good and evil in terms of love and hate:

> "*We all have experience of two types of feeling. There is the feeling which unites us to our world and makes us rejoice in it, an experience of love, of acceptance, of communion. And there is the other kind of feeling which separates us from our world and makes us hate it, an experience of fear, of exile, of discord. The first of these feelings belongs more truly to us than the second. We are profoundly satisfied by love and communion. We are exasperated by exile and hatred . . . The difference between these two types of feeling is the difference between* good *and* evil *and evil is secondary, existing not in its own right but as thwarted goodness.*"**

As I said in the first chapter, evil is understood today more in terms of an actual force rather than an abstract idea and perceived rather than conceived. When I saw a 'Hell's Angel' who asked for exorcism with the word 'Hate' tattooed on his arm, it made me recognise the force he was using. He described it in terms of a feeling, like a force gripping him, which he pleaded with me to remove.

Hitler's 'Hymn of Hate' is no exaggeration. Exorcism is not purely dealing with the occult or psychic phenomena; it is dealing with hate forces emanating from human beings, induced by

* Matt. 6: 23.
** TRUE WILDERNESS, Williams, p. 117.

Satan. 'God is love', and the 'Devil is hate', to put it crudely and so it is profound to interpret good and evil in terms of love and hate. If we are to answer the challenge as to whether we are servants of God or slaves of Satan, than it can only be answered by whether love or hate is predominant in our lives. One of the African students, as he left for Africa, told our Universal Prayer Group that he had learned *not* to hate.

Let us remember that hate is not purely virulent words or violent actions, but a deep seated harbouring of resentment and this can only be overcome by love. Joseph said to his brethren "Ye meant evil against me, but God meant it for good."* Their evil intent and hatred was wonderfully portrayed in the recent play "Joseph and the Amazing Technicolour Dreamcoat." Although they had shown hatred against him he showed them love and evil was overcome by good. This gracious love was also seen in the context of the play.

Let love abound

Let us remember also that love in the New Testament Greek is *αγαπη*,—a new concept, or perhaps percept, not the classical word *ερως* meaning romantic love. John Robinson describes it as 'unselfregarding love', Harry Williams describes it as 'generous self-giving love', Reinhold Neibuhr translates it as 'sacrificial love'. George Bernard Shaw once said "If you begin by sacrificing yourself to those you love, you will end by hating those to whom you have sacrified yourself."** This is a dangerous half-truth because it is a superficial judgement. Surely, sacrifice rightly motivated, transforms hate into love and overcomes evil with good. Love is indeed sacrificial because 'God commendeth his own love towards us that while we were yet sinners, Christ died for us'. Sacrifice, as Dr. Temple once said "is the open secret of the heart of God." It is through sacrifice, doing something for love's

* Gen. 50: 20.
** Revolutionist's Handbook in Man and Superman, Shaw.

sake which we would not do apart from love, which is in fact redemptive suffering. Through such love lives are re-created by the Spirit of God. The true servant of God is the 'servant of the servants of God'. One of the greatest servants of God was St. Francis and it is in his prayer that we find the true service of God, in the sacrificial offering of his whole life for God, a striking example of 'God's man for others'. For in this prayer of St. Francis we see how wonderfully lives can be re-created by the Spirit of God, using his servants as instruments of his purpose.

"*Lord, make me an instrument of your peace.*
Where there is hatred, let me sow love
Where there is injury, pardon
Where there is doubt, faith
Where there is despair, hope
Where there is darkness, light
Where there is sadness, joy
O Divine Master grant that I may not so much seek
to be consoled as to console
To be understood, as to understand
To be loved, as to love
For it is in giving that we receive
It is in pardoning that we are pardoned
It is in dying that we are born to eternal life."
"*Be not overcome of evil, but overcome evil with good.*"
Rom. 12: 21